Literary Disability Studies

Series Editors
David Bolt
Liverpool Hope University
Liverpool, UK

Elizabeth J. Donaldson
New York Institute of Technology
Old Westbury, NY, USA

Julia Miele Rodas
Bronx Community College
City University of New York
Bronx, NY, USA

Literary Disability Studies is the first book series dedicated to the exploration of literature and literary topics from a disability studies perspective. Focused on literary content and informed by disability theory, disability research, disability activism, and disability experience, the Palgrave Macmillan series provides a home for a growing body of advanced scholarship exploring the ways in which the literary imagination intersects with historical and contemporary attitudes toward disability. This cutting edge interdisciplinary work includes both monographs and edited collections (as well as focused research that does not fall within traditional monograph length). The series is supported by an editorial board of internationally-recognised literary scholars specialising in disability studies:

Michael Bérubé, Edwin Erle Sparks Professor of Literature, Pennsylvania State University, USA; G. Thomas Couser, Professor of English Emeritus, Hofstra University in Hempstead, New York, USA; Michael Davidson, University of California Distinguished Professor, University of California, San Diego, USA; Rosemarie Garland-Thomson, Professor of Women's Studies and English, Emory University, Atlanta, USA; Cynthia Lewiecki-Wilson, Professor of English Emerita, Miami University, Ohio, USA. For information about submitting a Literary Disability Studies book proposal, please contact the series editors: David Bolt (boltd@hope.ac.uk), Elizabeth J. Donaldson (elizabeth.donaldson@asu.edu), and/or Julia Miele Rodas (Julia.Rodas@bcc.cuny.edu).

Susannah B. Mintz • Gregory Fraser
Editors

Placing Disability

Personal Essays of Embodied Geography

Editors
Susannah B. Mintz
Skidmore College
Saratoga Springs, NY, USA

Gregory Fraser
University of West Georgia
Carrollton, GA, USA

ISSN 2947-7409 ISSN 2947-7417 (electronic)
Literary Disability Studies
ISBN 978-3-031-41218-9 ISBN 978-3-031-41219-6 (eBook)
https://doi.org/10.1007/978-3-031-41219-6

© The Editor(s) (if applicable) and The Author(s), under exclusive licence to Springer Nature Switzerland AG 2024

This work is subject to copyright. All rights are solely and exclusively licensed by the Publisher, whether the whole or part of the material is concerned, specifically the rights of translation, reprinting, reuse of illustrations, recitation, broadcasting, reproduction on microfilms or in any other physical way, and transmission or information storage and retrieval, electronic adaptation, computer software, or by similar or dissimilar methodology now known or hereafter developed.

The use of general descriptive names, registered names, trademarks, service marks, etc. in this publication does not imply, even in the absence of a specific statement, that such names are exempt from the relevant protective laws and regulations and therefore free for general use.

The publisher, the authors, and the editors are safe to assume that the advice and information in this book are believed to be true and accurate at the date of publication. Neither the publisher nor the authors or the editors give a warranty, expressed or implied, with respect to the material contained herein or for any errors or omissions that may have been made. The publisher remains neutral with regard to jurisdictional claims in published maps and institutional affiliations.

This Palgrave Macmillan imprint is published by the registered company Springer Nature Switzerland AG.
The registered company address is: Gewerbestrasse 11, 6330 Cham, Switzerland

Paper in this product is recyclable.

Acknowledgments

Our deepest thanks go to all of the writers included in this book. We began this project in the first winter of the COVID-19 pandemic, and we're grateful to our authors for their patience as we developed the collection and for the insights, surprises, and wisdom of their stories of embodiment in/and place. We acknowledge the diligence and painstaking quality of collaboration, and thank every contributor for their generosity throughout this process. Getting to know this extraordinary group of writers, on the page and in many emails over these past few years, has brought us much joy. Our thanks also go to Allie Troyanos at Palgrave Macmillan for her support. We're grateful, as always, to the academic departments, colleagues, friends, and family who facilitate the work we do as writers and scholars, from the dog walking we might've neglected when editorial tasks got overwhelming to the intellectual compassion and rigor that inspire and sustain us. We are enormously proud to usher the essays of *Placing Disability* into the world.

Contents

1 **Introduction**   1
Susannah B. Mintz and Gregory Fraser

2 **Disability and Memoir**   9
G. Thomas Couser

3 **Space, Place, and Disability**   17
Rob Imrie

Part I   Into the Wide Open   27

4 **Learning the Camino Real—Disability and the Desert**   29
Sheila Black

5 **Headlamps and Fireside Light**   41
Rachel Kolb

6 **A Sense of Place & Cyberspace: The Hybrid Way I Live, Work, and Play**   53
Gyasi Burks-Abbott

7 ***Ad Astra Per Aspera* (To the Stars Through Difficulties)**   61
Brenda Jo Brueggemann

Part II Metro-Geographies — 67

8 Peaks and Valleys: A Collaborative Essay about Disability in the Bronx — 69
Julia Miele Rodas, Sonia Gonzalez, Annette Serrano, Cindy Hernandez, Andrew Whyte, Jovan Campbell, and Mary Morfe

9 Blindness and Dyslexia in the Movements of Everyday Life in Toronto — 85
Rod Michalko and Tanya Titchkosky

10 Disability in New York City Schools and Preparing Teachers to Work in Them — 95
Laurie Rabinowitz

11 Drenched Lands, Blood Compost: Disability, Land, and The Asylum Project — 103
Petra Kuppers

Part III Liminal (Dis)locations — 113

12 A Tide in the River: Auditory Ecologies of Dyarubbin — 115
Nicole Matthews

13 Hydra, New Hampshire — 127
Stephen Kuusisto

14 Between Places — 131
Leigh A. Neithardt

15 The Lie of the Land — 139
Annmaree Watharow

16 Body Workers — 149
Ellen Samuels

17 Never in One Place: On Waking in a Different Body — 153
Anand Prahlad

Index — 165

Notes on Contributors

Sheila Black is the author of five poetry collections—*House of Bone*; *Love/Iraq*; *Wen Kroy* (winner of the Orphic Prize in Poetry); *Iron, Ardent*; and *Radium Dream*—and three chapbooks, most recently, *All the Sleep in the World* (Alabrava, 2021). Her poems and essays have appeared in *Poetry*, *Kenyon Review Online*, *Blackbird*, *The Birmingham Poetry Review*, *The New York Times*, and elsewhere. She is co-editor of *Beauty Is a Verb: The New Poetry of Disability* (Cinco Puntos, 2011), named a Notable Book for Adults by the American Library Association. In 2012, Black received a Witter Bynner Fellowship from the Library of Congress (selected by Philip Levine). She is a co-founder of Zoeglossia, a non-profit organization that builds community for poets with disabilities. She currently serves as assistant director of the Virginia G. Piper Center for Creative Writing in Tempe, AZ.

Brenda Jo Brueggemann is Professor of English, Women's, Gender, and Sexuality Studies, and American Studies at the University of Connecticut. She was the editor of *Disability Studies Quarterly* for ten years and is author or co-author of three published books and editor or co-editor of six published books. Her lifetime teaching and writing/publications have always centered on disability studies and deaf studies.

Gyasi Burks-Abbott is on the faculty of both the Leadership Education in Neurodevelopmental and Related Disabilities (LEND) Program at Boston Children's Hospital and the UMass Boston Institute for Community Inclusion. He graduated from Macalester College in St. Paul, MN, with a BA in English and psychology, and holds an MS in Library and Information Science from Simmons University in Boston. Burks-Abbott serves on the boards, committees, and commissions of many autism and disability organizations, and has written for several autism and disability-related publications. He tells the story of how he became an autism self-advocate in his autobiography, *My Mother's Apprentice: An Autistic's Rites of Passage* (Yorkshire, 2022).

Jovan Campbell is a disability and women's empowerment advocate, the co-founder of One Heart One Vision, and co-host of the One Heart One Vision podcast, which discusses the experiences of a disabled woman in a non-disabled world. Born in Brooklyn, NY, Campbell has diabetic retinopathy and chronic kidney disease, and is a partial wheelchair user. She is currently a Bronx resident, completing her Public Health degree at Bronx Community College.

G. Thomas Couser earned his doctorate in American Studies from Brown University in 1977. He taught at Connecticut College from 1976 to 1982, then at Hofstra University, where he founded the Disability Studies Program, until his retirement in 2011. Couser joined the faculty of the Narrative Medicine program at Columbia in 2021 and introduced a Disability Studies course to the curriculum in 2022. His academic books include *Recovering Bodies: Illness, Disability, and Life Writing* (Wisconsin, 1997), *Vulnerable Subjects: Ethics and Life Writing* (Cornell, 2004), *Signifying Bodies: Disability in Contemporary Life Writing* (Michigan, 2009), and *Memoir: An Introduction* (Oxford, 2012). In addition, he has published personal essays and *Letter to My Father: A Memoir* (Hamilton, 2017).

Gregory Fraser serves as Professor of English at the University of West Georgia, outside Atlanta. He is the author of four poetry collections: *Strange Pietà* (Texas Tech, 2003), *Answering the Ruins* (2009), *Designed for Flight* (2014), and *Little Armageddon* (2021), all from Northwestern University Press. He is also the co-author of the workshop textbook *Writing Poetry* (Palgrave Macmillan, 2008) and the critical-writing textbook *Analyze Anything* (Bloomsbury, 2012). Fraser's poetry, which often addresses themes of disability, illness, and place, has appeared in journals including *The New Yorker*, *The Paris Review*, *The Southern Review*, and *Ploughshares*. He is the recipient of several awards for his writing, including grants from the National Endowment for the Arts and the Guggenheim Foundation.

Sonia Gonzalez is a PhD candidate in English at the CUNY Graduate Center. Her research interests include disability theory and Latinx literature and culture. She lives in New York City with her husband, three children, and dog.

Cindy Hernandez is a graduate of Bronx Community College and plans to pursue a bachelor's degree in Thanatology. She loves writing, reading, drawing, and finding new challenges.

Rob Imrie was previously Professor of Sociology at Goldsmiths University of London, where he retains a Visiting Professorship. He has written widely on issues relating to architecture and urban design, urban policy and politics, and disability and the built environment. His latest book is *Concrete Cites: Why We Need to Build Differently* (Bristol, 2021).

Rachel Kolb is a Junior Fellow at the Harvard Society of Fellows. Her academic work on deafness and American literature has been published in *J19* and *The Journal of Literary and Cultural Disability Studies*, and her public scholarship has appeared in *The New York Times*, *The Atlantic*, *Poetry*, and TEDx Stanford.

Petra Kuppers is a disability culture activist and a community performance artist. Kuppers grounds herself in disability culture methods, using somatics, performance, and speculative writing to engage audiences toward more socially just and enjoyable futures. Her latest book is *Eco Soma: Joy and Pain in Speculative Performance Encounters* (Minnesota, 2022, open access). A 2023 Guggenheim Fellow, and a 2022 Dance/USA Fellow, Kuppers teaches at both the University of Michigan and Goddard College. (www.petrakuppers.com).

Stephen Kuusisto holds a University Professorship at Syracuse University. He is the author of the memoirs *Have Dog, Will Travel: A Poet's Journey; Planet of the Blind* (a *New York Times* Notable Book of the Year), and *Eavesdropping: A Memoir of Blindness and Listening*. His poetry collections include *Only Bread, Only Light; Letters to Borges; Old Horse, What Is To Be Done?*, and the forthcoming *Close Escapes: A Memoir in Verse*. Kuusisto travels and lectures widely on human rights, disability, literature, and the advantages of guide dogs and human-animal relationships.

Nicole Matthews teaches media and cultural studies at Macquarie University in Sydney, on the lands of the Wattamattagal people of the Darug nation. She writes essays and creative nonfiction, as well as academic articles on mediated autobiography, digital media, and visual culture, drawing on disability and deaf studies. Her most recent book, with Naomi Sunderland, is *Digital Storytelling in Health and Social Policy* (2017). Since 2020, she has had several solo exhibitions of her photographs of Dyarubbin/The Hawkesbury River.

Rod Michalko taught sociology and disability studies at several Canadian universities, including most recently the University of Toronto. Since his retirement, he has focused on writing fiction that features characters who are blind. Michalko has published numerous articles and books, including *The Mystery of the Eye and the Shadow of Blindness* (Toronto, 1998), *The Two in One: Walking with Smokie, Walking with Blindness* (Temple, 1999), and *The Difference that Disability Makes* (Temple, 2002). He is co-editor with Tanya Titchkosky of *Rethinking Normalcy: A Disability Studies Reader*. Michalko is also the author of the short story collection *Things are Different Here* (Insomniac, 2017) and *Letters with Smokie* (Manitoba, 2023, with Dan Goodley), which blends fiction and nonfiction to explore intersections of blindness, disability, and what it means to be human from the canine perspective of his late guide dog, Smokie.

Susannah B. Mintz is Professor of English at Skidmore College. Her books include the memoir *Love Affair in the Garden of Milton: Poetry, Loss, and the Meaning of Unbelief* (LSU, 2021) and four scholarly volumes on disability and literature, most recently *The Disabled Detective: Sleuthing Disability in Contemporary Crime Fiction* (Bloomsbury, 2019) and *Hurt and Pain: Literature and the Suffering Body* (2014). She is also the co-editor of four collections of work on disability issues, including *Disability in the Long Eighteenth Century* (2019, with Chris Gabbard) and *Disability Experiences* (2019, with G. Thomas Couser); work-in-progress includes *Hypochondria: Symptom or Story?* (Reaktion, 2024). Her creative nonfiction has won numerous awards and appears in the Notable list of *Best American Essays* and the *Pushcart Prize Anthology*. (www.susannahbmintz.com)

Mary Morfe serves as Alumni Advisor to the CUNY Coalition for Students with Disability at both Lehman College and Bronx Community College (BCC), providing support and guidance to student members. She also works for Lehman's Campus Information Services and for BCC as a College Assistant.

Leigh A. Neithardt is a scholar of children's literature and disability studies. A staff member at the Modern Language Association, she holds a PhD in teaching and learning and an MFA in creative writing. (www.leighneithardt.com)

Anand Prahlad is a Curators' Distinguished Teaching Professor Emeritus in the Department of English at the University of Missouri. He is a folklore scholar, literary author, disability activist, and musician. His scholarly works include *African-American Proverbs in Context* and *Reggae Wisdom: Proverbs in Jamaican Music*. The author of numerous journal articles, he edited *The Greenwood Encyclopedia of African American Folklore*. Prahlad's creative works include the poetry collections *As Good as Mango* and *Dreaming of Endangered Species*, and the disability memoir *The Secret Life of a Black Aspie*. His recent work employs frames of intersectionality, while focusing on black ancestry, gender-fluid identity, and transgenerational trauma.

Laurie Rabinowitz is an Assistant Professor of Education Studies at Skidmore College. She was previously a special-education teacher at a public school in Harlem, and a Director of Instruction at a New York City charter school. Her research explores inclusive practices and the intersections of literacy and inclusive pedagogy.

Julia Miele Rodas is Professor of English at Bronx Community College/City University of New York. She is a co-editor of the Literary Disability Studies book series (Palgrave Macmillan) and contributing co-editor for *The Madwoman and the Blindman:* Jane Eyre, *Discourse, Disability* (Ohio State, 2012). She is also the author of *Autistic Disturbances: Theorizing Autism Poetics from the* DSM *to* Robinson Crusoe (Michigan, 2018). Rodas is currently working on a project about violence and psychiatric disability, grounded in experiences from her own life.

Ellen Samuels is Professor of Gender & Women's Studies and English and founding member of the Disability Studies Initiative at the University of Wisconsin at Madison. Her books include *Fantasies of Identification: Disability, Gender, Race* (NYU, 2014) and *Hypermobilities: Poems* (Operating System, 2021). Her critical and creative writing has appeared in dozens of journals and anthologies, including *Signs, GLQ, South Atlantic Quarterly, Disability Studies Quarterly, Disability Visibility, Brevity,* and *The Massachusetts Review*. She is currently writing two books: *Double Meanings: Conjoined Twins and Cultural Resignification* and *Sick Time: What Chronic Life Tells Us*. (twitter @ehlastigirl).

Annette Serrano is a student at Bronx Community College, earning a degree in Human Services. Having adjusted to her own disability, Serrano has found her passion in helping others.

Tanya Titchkosky is a Disability Studies Professor in Social Justice Education at the University of Toronto. Her books include *Disability, Self, and Society* (2003), *Reading and Writing Disability Differently* (2007), and *The Question of Access: Disability, Space, Meaning* (2011), all from the University of Toronto Press. She is also the co-editor of *Rethinking Normalcy: A Disability Studies Reader* (2009, with Rod Michalko) and *DisAppearing: Encounters in Disability Studies* (2022), both from Canadian Scholars Press. Her work is supported by a Social Sciences and Humanities Research Council Grant. A recipient of the 2019 Distinguished Contributions to Teaching Award, Titchkosky is a participant in the international research project Disability Matters, where she examines how corporate health archives mediate the meaning of disability.

Annmaree Watharow holds a medical degree (1986), a master's degree in Psychological Medicine (1993), and a PhD (2021) that focuses on the hospital experiences of people living with sensory disabilities. A Lived Experience Fellow in the Centre for Disability Research and Policy at the University of Sydney, Watharow is currently developing a play that introduces the community to the experiences of people with sensory loss as they navigate the health care system, and has recently published *Improving the Experience of Health Care for People Living with Sensory Disability: Knowing What is Going On.*

Andrew Whyte is a psychology major at Bronx Community College, where he is studying to become a teacher or counselor. When he's not busy with school, Whyte enjoys drawing, journaling, and basketball, as well as spending time with his family, friends, and cat.

1

Introduction

Susannah B. Mintz and Gregory Fraser

Humans have been mapping the world since at least the ancient Babylonians. The earliest known cartographic representation dates from around 600 BCE. It is a three-by-five-inch clay tablet depicting the Earth as a flat disc surrounded by ocean; the Euphrates River is marked, as is the city of Babylon, along with wedge-shaped lands given purely descriptive names: "beyond the flight of birds" and "a place where the sun cannot be seen." Like many vellum and paper maps to follow, the Babylonian tablet combines what's already charted and what's wholly imagined, displaying both the limits of geographical exploration as well as ideas (and warnings) about the mysteries lying beyond those edges. The monsters and sea serpents that reared up from medieval European maps, for instance, not only served to delight readers' fancy, but also to alert seafarers to the dangers of unexplored reaches of the ocean. Such a map is a guide: if we orient properly, it will lead us to the right place. It also suggests possibilities. Drawing the world around us gives pictorial shape to the excitement of discovery as well as the satisfactions of familiarity, of identity. Whether we leave or stay home, to be located *here* is always to understand ourselves in some relation to whatever lies over *there*.

S. B. Mintz (✉)
Skidmore College, Saratoga Springs, NY, USA
e-mail: smintz@skidmore.edu

G. Fraser
University of West Georgia, Carrollton, GA, USA
e-mail: gfraser@westga.edu

© The Author(s), under exclusive license to Springer Nature Switzerland AG 2024
S. B. Mintz, G. Fraser (eds.), *Placing Disability*, Literary Disability Studies,
https://doi.org/10.1007/978-3-031-41219-6_1

It may seem inevitable that old-style *mappa mundi*—drawn before the supposed objectivity of complex projection science—would distort sizes and distances in favor of the mapmakers' positionality. But so-called map bias pertains even to the Mercator Projection world maps that have adorned European and North American classrooms for hundreds of years. Given the impossibility of accurately representing the contours of a sphere on a flat, rectangular piece of paper—to say nothing of continual territory and border disputes—two-dimensional maps *mis*-represent by definition, and cartographers make choices about what to privilege: directionality, for example, as did Gerardus Mercator in 1569, over shape and size. It's by now well understood that the Mercator map enlarges the size of Greenland and shrinks that of Africa, though many will still visualize the globe—and so potentially make assumptions about "importance"—according to the spatial relations of the Mercator portrayal. Power, favoritism, ideological preconceptions: these are embedded in what we've been given to see as accurate, neutral pictures of the world. [1]

Writers map the world in ways that have tended to a different type of apparent universality. Consider the long tradition of colonial travel writing, in which intrepid explorers bring back tales of exotic climes, foods, rituals, and bodies to readers eager to be both titillated and reassured of their inherently rightful place as guardians of civilization. Such work reinforces social and cultural inequity as a matter of geography. Or to put this differently, travel writers render geography as inherently embodied, to the degree that a sense of a landscape is determined by the people who populate it and by a traveler's physical encounter with it: how it is seen, perambulated, heard, cogitated upon; how we come to know ourselves and others within it.

So too does a great deal of writing from home—from where we *are* and not just where we've *been*—concretize attitudes about the self in relation to how bodies move through space. The figure of the *flâneur* who emerged in nineteenth-century French literature was one who mapped the urban grid of Paris by simultaneously strolling and watching as a keen, full-body observer of social mores and habits. Virginia Woolf's 1927 essay "Street Haunting" takes up the *flâneur*'s brand of metropolitan spectatorship in London to raise questions about who we are behind the windows and curtains—metaphorically, but also literally—of storefronts. Much later, Joan Didion would memorialize Manhattan in her extraordinary renunciation of it in "Goodbye to All That" (1967), an essay that indulges the pleasure of walking the city at dawn as exemplary of a youthful expressiveness the writer no longer enjoys. These works depend for their psychological impact on the ambulatory and visual perspectives of their narrators, although neither Didion, Woolf, nor Baudelaire before them comments on that physical capacity—it is simply taken for granted. These are works of enormous significance in the genealogy of creative nonfiction. They are also, inherently, ableist.

* * *

Ableism is defined as an ideology of preference for healthy, functioning bodyminds. It assumes the *obviousness* of the belief that able-bodied/mindedness is always to be preferred over the alternative and takes impairment of any sort as a defect compromising subjectivity. From that obviousness derive attitudes and policies that discredit the humanity of disabled people. The medical model, the dominant conceptual paradigm in Western thinking about embodiment since the eighteenth century, has defined impairment as a problem of individual bodies, often a catastrophic one, that needs to be cured, corrected, or rehabilitated in order to restore the status of full personhood. By contrast, the social model has over the past half century shifted focus toward questions of social location and interaction. According to this approach, "disability" is what happens when bodily or cognitive/psychiatric difference encounters an inhospitable environment; far from a tragic personal loss or lack, it is instead a function of what Rosemarie Garland-Thomson (2011) has referred to as the "misfit" between anomalous bodies and minds and cultural norms. We now understand disability as both a minority identity and as a vital source of knowledge in its own right. The term "cripistemology" has come to refer to ways of knowing, and to forms of creative expression, that originate from the perspective of illness or impairment and so resist conventional paradigms.

The social model's emphasis on the built environment (and the biases that undergird its design) has compelled our attention to questions of access and to the incompatibility between certain kinds of spaces and atypical modes of thought or movement. On a college campus, we might be fighting not just for automatic doors that actually open or reliable notetakers in class, but also against notions of success that privilege intellectual speed and productivity or that demand we comport ourselves interactionally in specific ways. A useful counterpoint is then a city like Berkeley, CA, birthplace of the Independent Living Movement and one of the most physically and attitudinally accessible spaces in the US; Berkeley dramatically gives the lie to any prejudice equating impairment to diminishment or helplessness. In these contexts, it's easy to understand how "disability" is brought into being by environments—whether through stigma, physical layouts that privilege nondisabled bodyminds, or the myriad unarticulated, normative codes that govern our daily behaviors and interactions.

But there are other reasons that a person growing up in California might experience disability quite differently from someone whose hometown is Toronto, Sydney, or Prague—or rural New Hampshire, the suburban Midwest, or the southwestern desert. We become who we are in landscapes and topographies that influence us whether or not they are openly hostile to our ways of moving, sensing, thinking, and feeling. As those early cartographers understood, figuring out where we are is a way of saying *why* we are: not only in geopolitical terms, but also in more intimate, prosaic, ruminative, even comical moments of engagement with the places where we live. The quality of the light, for example, or the presence of water, the degree of ambient noise, the yearly aggravation of snow and ice, the nearness of neighbors, the spaciousness of sky—what effect do these have on our particular forms of embodiment? What we see and hear; how the ground beneath us, the river around us, support or defy our movements; whether we feel eager to go out or inclined to stay in: this too is embodied geography. What then is meaningful to being, or becoming, disabled—and to *claiming* disability—in the terrains we inhabit? What is the geo-logic—with respect to disability—of cities, shorelines, farms, even cyberspace?

When we meet someone new, we ask questions we hope will elicit information that helps us situate that person in recognizable narratives of identity. Both make assumptions about the correlation between personality and the kinds of spaces we occupy. "What do you do?" (or as students are keen to amend, "What do you *plan* to do?") presumes that something fundamental to our characters is revealed by the kinds of jobs we choose—in addition to reinforcing an entrenched correspondence between social legitimacy and economic value that has historically disadvantaged people with disabilities. "Where are you from?" implies some similarly pithy encapsulation of a person's intrinsic qualities based on the ethos of place. Both queries try to sum up a stranger without a lot of fuss—to "know" them without probing too deeply into the crevasses of psyche. But that's not all the work such questions perform, since both are also points of entry that might introduce us to less expected convergences of environment and subjectivity. As the authors in this collection investigate, everything that we *do*, in all the senses of that verb, takes shape somewhere. The journeys they recount map the world anew: interrogating, elegizing, and celebrating according to and not in willful neglect of disability, seeking out the variousness, the urgency and gorgeousness, of human experience on a vulnerable and most extraordinary Earth.

* * *

Current scholarly work on disability and the environment focuses largely on architecture and spatial theory or affinities between eco-criticism and literary disability analysis. Disability scholarship on space also tends to be theoretical rather than experiential, focused on space in philosophical terms rather than specific geographies. The essays in *Placing Disability* expand on such work by situating authors' reflections on the meaning of embodiment in distinct physical places and by grounding the discourse of disability awareness and activism in personal experience. We intend this collection to be useful in creative-writing workshops, Disability Studies seminars, and classes on environmental literature, and to appeal to general readers of memoir as well as to scholars of contemporary body theory or the Anthropocene.

Writer and activist Eli Clare, who lives in the Green Mountains of Vermont, provides an example of the kind of thinking that undergirds this collection. In *Brilliant Imperfection* (2017), Clare narrates what happens when he hits a "steep stretch" on a mountain hike, given his unsteady "relationship to gravity":

> I yearn to fly downhill, feet touching ground, pushing off... Instead... I drop down onto my butt and slide along using both my hands and feet... Only then do I see the swirl marks that glaciers left in the granite, tiny orange newts climbing among the tree roots, otherworldly fungi growing on rotten logs. My shaky balance gives me this intimacy with the mountain. (88)

Clare is not the first nature essayist to demonstrate the epistemological benefits of reorienting ourselves toward the environment (Camille Dungy and Terry Tempest Williams come to mind), but here the perspective is a disabled one, as disability becomes the condition for knowing the world as well as for the prose that emerges from such discovery. In this pointed instance of cripistemology, disability is figured as the mode of knowing the environment just as the experience of being disabled is directly shaped by the contours of the landscape.

Clare challenges social injustice as an activist and intellectual, *and* as a memoirist. Memoir is not the only literary form with the potential to change our minds, but the sense of "reality" that pertains to autobiographical work—the immediacy, honesty, and self-disclosure that are its hallmarks—grant to nonfiction a dynamic effect that operates on us as readers. We turn to particular nonfictionists for the pleasure of their company—for the sense of being informed, guided, even comforted by someone who has pondered the thickets of difficult experience with diligent self-awareness, this one wry and gritty, that one quietly lyrical, still a third perhaps mixing a personal with an academic or professional register. In that conviction of getting the true story of experience, readers may be open to redirection.

Like Clare, the writers in *Placing Disability* propose that disability identity cannot be divorced from location. The collection presents a series of "geo-cripistemologies," as authors explore issues of movement, work and play, community and activism, artistic production, love and marriage, access and social services, family and friendship, memory and aging—all informed by the places they inhabit. The essays themselves represent a new kind of rhetorical geography as authors combine personal, lyrical, auto-critical, and neo-academic modes to tell their stories of how spaces and disabilities come mutually into being. The book is organized in terms of topographies and vistas, rather than being bound by the map, to emphasize the kinds of experiences that happen in places (whatever they look, smell, or feel like)—experiences that authors render in terms of their defining, constitutive effects.

The collection begins with two brief overviews. The first, by G. Thomas Couser, reviews the history of disability memoir and its importance to the ongoing efforts of the disability rights movement. The next, by Rob Imrie, examines the politicization of space and its constricting, sometimes violent effects on people with disabilities, as well as innovations in spatial design that promote access, safety, and enjoyment. The subsequent essays are grouped in three conceptual sections. In Part 1, "Into the Wide Open," authors explore the interplay of solitude and connection in expansive, sometimes frightening spaces—the southwestern desert, a midwestern farm, the woods and wilderness, and digital space—that unexpectedly facilitate communication, joy, and understanding. In Part 2, "Metro-geographies," authors traverse urban spaces, navigating density, disparity, noise, uneven ground, and the institutions located there as a complex encounter with touch, pain, memory, companionship, instruction, and the past. The essays in Part 3, "Liminal (Dis)locations," recount experiences of bodily risk and discovery at the edges of spaces (New England treetops and tall grass, Australian harbors and rivers, the interpersonal space of body work, spaces forgotten by nondisabled society, an oak beyond the window of a midwestern house in a fractious America), considering the kinds of responsibility to and care of others that the landscape can teach us how to foster.

The twenty-four authors included in *Placing Disability* hail from different countries, neighborhoods, climates, and landscapes; from various backgrounds and professions; from a range of disciplinary perspectives and strategies. They are trained as social scientists, academics, literary critics, poets, musicians, students, public speakers, memoirists, folklorists, educators, rhetoricians, philosophers, librarians, administrators, and activists. Their essays refine our understanding of the complex dynamic between self and circumstance as they survey the impact of geographical region on their life experiences. They resist the pressure to draw conclusions or declare priorities, but instead negotiate a plethora of landscapes, contemplating the realities they afford, and reminding us that *where* disability happens matters to *what* disability means for our collective grasp of the human condition.

Note

1. In 2017, the Boston, MA school district began to phase out the Mercator Projection map in favor of the lesser-known Peters Projection. It was the first school district in the U.S. to do so.

Works Cited

Clare, Eli. 2017. *Brilliant Imperfection: Grappling with Cure*. Durham, NC: Duke University Press.

Garland-Thomson, Rosemarie. 2011. "Misfits: A Feminist Materialist Disability Concept." *Hypatia* 26 (3): 591–609.

2

Disability and Memoir

G. Thomas Couser

Today, memoir is the favored term for what used to be called autobiography. Or rather, it's the term for the currently most fashionable and critically acclaimed form of autobiography: the narrative of some single aspect of a living person's life, usually but not necessarily *by* that person. Thus, one can write a *biography* of anyone, an *autobiography* only of oneself, but a *memoir* of oneself or someone one knows. The single aspect can be a slice (a discrete period) or a thread—a theme, issue, or relationship. Either way, memoir lends itself well to narratives of disabling conditions, acute or chronic.

But only recently has disability been deemed an appropriate subject for memoir. Indeed, disability was rarely the primary focus of memoir until the last quarter of the twentieth century. A crucial decade was the 1990s, when HIV/AIDS prompted many life narratives in various genres, especially postmortem memorials of partners, sons, or brothers. Narratives of other conditions, like breast cancer and depression, also proliferated. When Susannah Mintz and I co-edited *Disability Experiences: Memoirs, Autobiographies, and Other Personal Narratives* (2019), a GaleCengage reference volume surveying the literature, we included some precursors of contemporary memoir, but were we to graph the narratives chronologically, the resulting image would be a sharply rising curve reflecting the memoir boom of the turn of the twenty-first century.

G. T. Couser (✉)
Hofstra University, Hempstead, NY, USA
e-mail: G.T.Couser@hofstra.edu

Factors accounting for this boom are many and diverse: changing attitudes toward the body; the wellness movement; feminism; gay and lesbian pride movements; the recognition of patients' rights, including access to their charts; and last, but hardly least, the disability rights movement, which gathered force in the 1970s and produced the Americans with Disabilities Act (ADA) in 1990. Indeed, in the U.S. and the U.K., at least, disability memoir has grown in rough synchrony with the Disability Rights Movement, in a reciprocal dynamic: disability awareness has enabled disability memoir, and vice versa. But whatever the causes, the result has been the burgeoning of a distinct body of literature, which I have called the *some body memoir*: the narrative of living with, in, or as a body that deviates from somatic norms. Indeed, the so-called memoir boom of the late twentieth century was in large part a function of the emergence of the some body memoir.

A curious feature of this surge is the distribution of narratives across the broad range of possible conditions. The 200 narratives surveyed in *Disability Experiences* depict about 100 conditions, ranging alphabetically from addiction, albinism, and Alzheimer's to Tourette syndrome, traumatic brain injury, and vision impairment. But the narratives are not evenly dispersed among these many conditions. Quite the contrary, a small number of conditions (e.g., depression, breast cancer, eating disorders, and autism) have produced a disproportionately large number of memoirs, while many conditions have produced only a small number. (A very few seem not to have produced any memoirs at all, but it's harder and harder to identify such exceptions.) The reasons for the currency of some conditions are not always clear, but this hierarchy obviously reflects latent cultural priorities, not the incidence of the conditions in question.

I have often lauded autobiography, or memoir, as the most democratic literary genre because it has historically served as a threshold form for minority communities—immigrants, Blacks, Native Americans, gays and lesbians, and so on. In recent decades, the disability memoir has confirmed this dynamic: somatic variation is yet another form of diversity embraced by this egalitarian genre. Because publishing gatekeepers today welcome the some body memoir, all one needs to claim the role of memoirist is a distinctively atypical body.

Of course, not all impairments are equal, or equally narratable, at least by the person experiencing them. Thus, an issue that distinguishes disability from other minority statuses is that some impairments inhibit, or even preclude, self-representation. For example, individuals with severe cognitive deficits, especially children, may be incapable of representing themselves; they may even be incapable of giving informed consent to their representation by others, such as their parents or siblings. The same is true at the end of the life span, when parents with dementia may be represented by care-giving adult children. Such individuals may be patronized, reduced to objects of pity, or characterized as burdens on a family or society at large. (There is a small but important body of narratives of assisted suicide.) In any case, they are vulnerable to representation that is not sanctioned by them or beneficial to them. So the third-person representation of people with disabilities in memoir is fraught with ethical dangers.

At the same time, the limits on self-representation by people with disabilities are less absolute than one might think. A notable aspect of the disability memoir boom has been pioneering memoirs by people with conditions such as Down syndrome, early-stage dementia, and autism. As recently as a couple of decades ago, respected scholars regarded autistic autobiography as a contradiction in terms: if a person were truly autistic, they wouldn't be capable of the necessary introspection and self-reflection. Yet today, bookstore shelves groan under memoirs by individuals "on the spectrum." Memoirs like these are performative utterances: their very existence communicates an important message.

But two aspects of the burgeoning of the some body memoir qualify its apparent inclusivity. One is that, like most literary composition, memoir-writing is a class-bound activity. Except in the important case of collaborative memoir, it requires a certain degree of literacy, which in turn depends on access to education (not to mention the free time to write). The recent advent of the graphic memoir would seem to lower the literacy threshold, narrowly considered, but it too requires education and leisure; and, if anything, it is probably more labor-intensive to produce. Consider this a "vertical" qualifier: the less privileged are less likely to produce memoir. And given the reciprocal causal links between disability and poverty, published memoirs of disabling conditions tend to depict relatively rare and benign scenarios. They may be authentic self-representation, but they are not broadly representative of the disabled population.

A related qualifier is geographical. In editing *Disability Experiences*, Susannah Mintz and I were encouraged to be geographically inclusive (with the caveat that the works needed to be available in English). But if we were to plot our narratives on a world map, the great majority would be found in the Global North. Indeed, disability memoir is popular (in both senses: prevalent and acclaimed) only in the Anglophone world, especially in the United States, where modern biomedicine and other cultural developments (among them prenatal screening) have made serious disability less common, hence more noteworthy and worthy of narration. Even within the Global North, cultural attitudes toward disability vary enormously from country to country. (Local geography varies dramatically, too, as this volume recognizes.)

In the Global South, where disability is more commonplace, it is regarded as mundane and therefore less worthy of narration. Also, disability rights and accommodation are rarer there; lacking such legal and cultural support, people with disabilities languish. They are less likely to live lives "worthy" of memoir, and more likely to lack the socioeconomic wherewithal to write and publish memoir. Thus, ironically, disability memoir is most common where disability is least common, and vice versa. Memoir may be a democratic genre, but disability memoir is still inaccessible in much of the world. Like its class distribution, then, the geographical distribution of disability memoir is very uneven.

In modern affluent societies that support disability rights (primarily the Anglosphere), impairment calls attention to itself and begs to be narrated. Indeed, disabled individuals are prone to being asked literally to account for themselves—by friends, acquaintances, or even passersby: "What happened to *you*?" Even when not spoken, the question is latent in the cultural environment. The preferred answer, however, is a story reassuring to the audience, one that does not threaten or implicate them. Impairments often carry a stigma or an implicit narrative; therefore, disabled subjects are sometimes in effect pre-inscribed. For example, people with lung cancer (a rarely narrated condition) are assumed to be heavy smokers. And during the AIDS epidemic, gay men were sometimes distinguished from "innocent victims" who contracted the virus through transfusion rather than sex.

So memoir may be open to disabled people "on condition"; access may be less open than it appears; and disability memoir can reinscribe ableist cultural discourse. The reading public may prefer narratives in which disabled people overcome their impairment: public acclaim may be reserved for stories of achieving something extraordinary, like climbing mountains while blind or on prosthetic legs. Such narratives may be popular, but they are disparaged by those in Disability Studies as "inspiration porn," because they reassure their readers (especially *non*disabled ones) that disabled people can do anything if they only try hard enough. Such stories focus on the individual to the exclusion of the environmental factors that are often more limiting than bodily impairments—for example, inaccessible buildings, lack of public transportation, and so on. They remove stigma from the heroic "supercrip" rather than from the impairment itself.

A key aspect of the Disability Rights Movement has been the adoption of the social paradigm by disability activists. This paradigm defines impairment and disability in counterintuitive ways. The term *impairment* refers to a feature of the body that differs from the norm: for instance, a spinal cord injury (SCI) that results in paraplegia or quadriplegia. The term *disability* is reserved for features of the environment that are disadvantageous to impaired bodies. The classic example is the absence of ramps, which limits the mobility of wheelchairs used by those with SCI. But disability refers to *any* limiting aspect of the individual's environment, whether attitudinal (ableism, fat phobia) or legal (inadequate enabling legislation). The social paradigm, then, performs a figure-ground reversal, shifting the focus from the impaired body to its social, political, and cultural context. By foregrounding the environment, physical as well as social, it calls out for memoirs rooted in particular geographies or architectural contexts (urban vs. rural), not to mention institutional (the workplace, the asylum).

Adopting the social paradigm, many disability memoirs expose the social and cultural obstacles to the masses of people with disabilities, rather than celebrating isolated achievements by exceptional (and often economically privileged) individuals. The social paradigm may be evident in the attention devoted to environmental limitations on the life of the ordinary disabled person, as it is in *Being Heumann* (2020), Judith Heumann's memoir of her lifelong activism. It may even be the explicit subject of memoirs, like those of Disability Studies scholars Simi Linton (*My Body Politic*, 2005), Georgina Kleege (*Sight Unseen*, 1999), and Steven Kuusisto (*Planet of the Blind*, 1997). These are clearly more progressive, more liberatory than memoirs that view disability through the medical paradigm, as a deficiency of the individual body. Indeed, many openly embrace and affirm disability as an integral part of the authors' identity. Some, in fact, take the form of "coming out" narratives.

But the social paradigm has been justly criticized for suppressing testimony about impairment itself: the experience of pain, fatigue, and physical deterioration that are intrinsic in some disabilities (as distinct from the disabling aspects of the environment, which are extrinsic). In response, recent years have seen a rise in memoirs of conditions like fibromyalgia (or Chronic Fatigue Syndrome), chronic Lyme disease, rheumatoid arthritis, and so on. Surely, the near future will see the publication of narratives of long COVID. So disability memoir now offers a platform for this somatic testimony, as well.

In any case, in recent decades, disabled people have seized upon the implicit cultural prompt to generate their own stories. This favors the disability community as a whole, as well those individuals who seek to narrate and publish their lives. And one of the virtues of the genre, as I see it, is precisely its openness to the experience of somatic variability, including its unpleasant facets. The disability memoir does not just advance the work of disability rights. It also does the work of reclaiming our somatic experience from the limitations of biomedical terminology and the medical gaze, which can be alien and alienating.

One of the great virtues of disability memoir is that it may resolve the perplexing phenomenon known as the "disability paradox." Social science has established that disabled people rate their own quality of life (QOL) about the same as nondisabled people rate theirs; in contrast, *non*disabled people estimate the QOL of disabled people as significantly inferior to their own. The apparent discrepancy between having a significant impairment and reporting good QOL is known as the "disability paradox." (It's not a true paradox, merely a counterintuitive truth, but nondisabled people view it as a contradiction in terms.) One way to understand it is to realize that estimations of the QOL of disabled people by nondisabled people tend to be skewed by their hypothetical nature: the stigma of disability is such that when nondisabled persons are asked to estimate the QOL of a disabled person, they tend to downgrade it on the basis of that single factor, which is, after all, the only thing they know about the hypothetical individual. In contrast, disabled people, and those who know them personally, rate their QOL more highly; they experience impairment as only one among many factors that contribute to their QOL. The key here is that self-reports are inherently holistic, whereas others' estimates are one-dimensional. In any case, the next best thing to knowing a person with a disability is knowing their story, in all its dimensions, through the medium of life writing. Disability memoirs can subtly convey the counterintuitive sense that disabled people have of their high QOL. (So I have been impelled to dub it "quality-of-life-writing.") This is certainly true of narratives like Harriet McBryde Johnson's *Too Late to Die Young* (2005), which relates the memoirist's pleasure in being bathed by her caregiver. Similarly, Georgina Kleege suggests that losing her sight in some ways enriched her experience of visual art, by requiring her to view it by scanning it close up. In any case, for both, disability brought a rewarding sense of community with other disabled people. For these reasons and in these ways, contemporary life writing more fully and fairly represents people with disabilities than ever before.

Works Cited

Heumann, Judith. 2020. *Being Heumann: An Unrepentant Memoir of a Disability Rights Activist*. Boston: Beacon Press.

Johnson, Harriet McBryde. 2005. *Too Late to Die Young: Nearly True Tales from a Life*. New York: Henry Holt.

Kleege, Georgina. 1999. *Sight Unseen*. New Haven: Yale Univ. Press.

Kuusisto, Steven. 1997. *Planet of the Blind*. New York: Dial.
Linton, Simi. 2005. *My Body Politic: A Memoir*. Ann Arbor: University of Michigan Press.
Thomas Couser, G., and Susannah B. Mintz, eds. 2019. *Disability Experiences: Memoirs, Autobiographies, and Other Personal Narratives*. Detroit: St. James Press (GaleCengage).

3

Space, Place, and Disability

Rob Imrie

A major challenge for disabled people is navigating through places often designed with little regard for a person's body and their physiological and emotional needs. Anne—a collaborator with me in a project about access and disability, and a person with multiple sclerosis—was a wheelchair user who found it difficult to access her local shops because of a lack of curb cuts and the presence of stairs. Her independence was compromised by insensitively designed spaces, which meant that she rarely went out and was primarily dependent on her children to run errands for her. For autistic people, environments are a profusion of sensory stimuli and overloads—from the noise of traffic, to crowds, to cluttered, disorganized urban spaces—all of which can be overwhelming and make everyday living next to impossible. In both instances, the production of space, including the design of buildings, pavements, and related infrastructure, fails to account for bodily diversity, a major challenge in seeking to create a more equitable and fairer world.

The design of our environments, rarely the purview of the general public, is usually left to professionals or groups that may lack the knowledge and understanding of how our bodies interact with the different spaces and places we inhabit. This is significant because it means that much of the environment is disabling or unable to respond to the multiple and diverse emotional and physiological needs that people have. Where things are, and how they connect

R. Imrie (✉)
Goldsmiths University of London, London, UK
e-mail: rob.imrie@gold.ac.uk

and relate to one another, is intrinsic to people's lives; our location, or where we are in a place, can affect our quality of life and opportunities to be part of society. As we can discern from the example of Anne, the design of a place, including the objects emplaced within it, shapes what we can do and how we can live: this includes vision-impaired people (whose capacities to function depend, in part, on the provision of non-visual cues or means of navigation) and deaf or hearing-impaired people (who experience exclusion from places because the design of environments privileges the "normal" hearing body).

That visual and aural cues are often missing is indicative of the debilitating and disabling characteristics of space, in which many bodies are rendered inert or unable to interact with/in the normalizing forms and features of the environment. This is characterized by the absence of legible spaces or places that fail to provide signs and signifiers, or the means to assure ease of interpretation of, and movement through, the environment. For the American designer Kevin Lynch, the illegibility of a space refers to the lack of "match between place and whole patterns of behavior," in which the prevalent culture—or "expectation, norms, and customary way of doing things"—is antithetical to physiological and mental differences in society (1981, 151). A potential outcome is the production of spaces that are, for some, uncomfortable and incongruous, or places that are ill-fitting, such that the body is potentially rendered less than able and out of place.

This dislocation between the body and space draws attention to the settings that bodies inhabit, and much can be learned about disability and the processes of disablement through a focus on these interrelationships. For Lynch, space is characterized by many misfitting or "movement hindered" features that bring about "hesitation, stumbling, blockage, embarrassment, accident, evident discomfort" (1981, 153). One of my research participants, Reiko, a vision-impaired person living in Tokyo, describes the debilitating nature of materials in the city this way: "I get to know places I walk around and I can easily navigate, but things can quickly change as objects, like cars, might be placed on pavements, or things have been moved around, and what I knew about the place becomes less certain."[1] Reiko's encounters with the ever-changing materiality of the city were a process of constantly re-learning her environment in a context whereby her body, in Maurice Merleau-Ponty's terms, had otherwise "ceased to be a knowing body" (1962, 329).

Reiko's experiences—her continuous remaking of her sense of the spaces that she moves through and her adaptation to them—illustrate the making of places as part of a reiterative social practice. For Reiko, space never stands still; it requires her to intervene and actively shape it as part of a process to guarantee freedom of movement and life itself. This perspective contrasts with a widely held, yet flawed, understanding of spatial relations as pre-formed, or as Bryan Reynolds and Joseph Fitzpatrick suggest, "space as the discursive circumstances that precede and therefore constitute the subject" (1999, 65). This imagines space as prior to its human occupation in which people do not exist and act without first being in place. There is the danger of conceiving place as determinant or able to exercise power over those objects or things that constitute it. In relation to the human body, the implication is that its emplacement may be regarded as no more than passive and reactive, and unable to exercise agency.

Reiko does not understand it this way; for her, space is not a given or fixed, and while physical fixtures may limit her movement and navigation, these are surmountable as she seeks to reassemble her cognitive senses of the changing environments. As Reiko recounts, "my movement through the streets is always altering and changing what I feel and I am able, at times, to make it easy enough for myself to move around . . . but, I'm always having to adjust and adapt to where I go to." This sense of her body as intertwined with space and the places she moves through is what Michel de Certeau (1984) describes as "ontogenetic," or something not fixed but fluid and changing—always in the making and shaped by the interactions between subjects and the environment. This is the constitutive making of place as a locale that, as Charles Withers suggests, reflects "the importance of the lived experiences and embodied practices there, and not somewhere else" (2009, 658).

While Reiko is hinting at the power of human agency to transform space, or the making of place as a relational practice, such powers are circumscribed and shaped by the socio-cultural context of space. Thomas Gieryn argues that place-making is "imbricated in moral judgments" (2000, 480), referring to the dominance of bodily norms rarely sensitized to impairment and the diverse physiologies of disabled people. These sentiments draw attention to the purposive production of space or, in Ed Soja's words, the "relations of power and discipline . . . inscribed into the apparently innocent spatiality of social life" (1989, 6). This is the often taken-for-granted nature of socio-spatial relations—the embodiment of normality or the able body in contrast to impairment and disability as not-normal. Here, the dualistic notion of the body, as abled or not, shapes the landscapes of disablement and is formative in propagating what Robert McRuer calls "compulsory able-bodiedness" (2002, 88), where the reproduction of the able body as the natural embodiment of space shifts disability to the margins.

These omnipresent margins come to the fore in the multiplicity of spaces to which disabled people are denied access, and where bodily prohibitions, both physical and cultural, are enacted. One significant margin relates to wild places, environments beyond the city, or spaces conceived as natural and off-limits to all but those with the able bodily means to access them. This connects the notion of nature and the natural with the able body, and suggests that bodies defined as disabled have no place in wild areas. Such is the powerful message of Alison Kafer's work, which describes popular discourses about nature that conceive of the authentic experience of wild areas as the walking, fit, body, while denigrating assistive technologies such as motorized wheelchairs (2017). These devices are conceived as anti-nature, undermining the purity of the wild environment. Yet, as Kafer notes, this "exclusionary framing of nature" misrepresents the ways in which paths and trails are socially constructed, not for all but in the image of those who conform to able-bodiedness (2017, 207).

The power of the compulsory able body pervades and shapes every aspect of society, denying disabled people the right to exist in the way that they would otherwise choose. One example is a recent debate between cyclists about the merits of including riders on organized long-distance events using electronic or battery-assisted cycles. An important part of geographical presence is mobility and movement, and the cycle is, potentially, a liberating machine. However, in the U.K., the prevalent attitude towards the use of assistive devices is ambivalent, with some people reluctant to include those who ride such machines. In a recent online exchange, a member of the Cycling Association involved in the debate expressed a regret: "I'm a Life Member—but due to a medical condition I may have to give up riding a 'normal' bike. I'd be so sad to no longer be able to ride events with my hubby and friends nor be part of the cycling community."

The potential marginalization of people who use assistive technologies for cycling, or for accessing wild and rural spaces, amounts to spatial injustice, which Ed Soja describes as the unfair and inequitable "distribution in space of socially valued resources and opportunities to use them" (2009, 2). Unjust geographies pervade every place, reflecting an underlying societal aversion to the impaired body that often translates into "no-go" spaces or environs where to be in place, within a particular body, is akin to aberrant behavior—some transgression and challenge to the moral order and conduct of society. State policy often revolves around the disciplining of transgressive bodies, including what Kafer calls "curative" (2013) or therapeutic interventions that detain disabled people in architectural spaces or places of carceral control. For instance, Linda Roslyn Steele documents the indefinite detention of disabled Indigenous persons in Australia, and argues that "disability makes space carceral" (2021, 94) because of legal and other social controls, from detention in institutions to guardianship and civil mental-health orders.

The endemic nature of disablism and carceral spaces in society is also manifest in what Claire Edwards and Nicola Maxwell refer to as the "diverse affectual and sensory geographies of un/safety" (2021, 157). Disabled people are at great risk of violence and hate crime, since being out in the world, in whatever spaces, entails the potential for hostility that revolves around associations with the impaired body as transgressive. Ed Hall, for instance, recounts a situation in which a disabled person was verbally abused in a car park for not parking in the designated accessible parking bay: "a man shouted at her, calling her 'a stupid fucking spastic' for taking up the extra space" (2019, 253). A research participant that I interviewed, a vision-impaired person, operated under a nightly curfew for fear of violence: "I won't go out at night because the lighting is too bad and it's intimidating. I got mugged and beaten to pulp a few months ago. Three youths did it, and they found them but didn't prosecute them" (qtd. in Imrie and Kumar, 1998, 362).

Such shocking encounters provide insights into what Edwards and Maxwell describe as "the situated, socio-spatial contexts and dynamics of such events" (2021, 159). This draws attention to the interrelationships between the physical and cultural characteristics and norms of space, disability, and the production of safe/unsafe places. For Edwards and Maxwell, space per se is not unsafe, but becomes so through the assemblage of "physical environments, temporal contexts, prior socialization and experiences, [and] societal discourses around disability" (2021, 159). These observations helpfully direct attention to the production of space and the contingent nature of place-based experiences such as the unpredictable street experiences of the vision-impaired participant I worked with: "I get different reactions to my white cane when I'm out. Some see it as an opportunity to hurl abuse, and others are helpful and give assistance" (Imrie and Kumar, 1998, 362). This is suggestive of the specific or situated nature of place, or the emplaced ways in which disability is enacted and reveals itself.

Beyond such experiences, place is much more than the material, object, world, or a location or point, but is also the affective attachments or relations we have to particular places. Withers notes that humanistic geographers conceive of place less "as a fractional unit of space" and more as a way of "being in the world" (2009, 640). This reflects a sense of place as an emotional attachment, or what Edward Relph defines as "profound centers of human existence" (1976, 43). This understanding is at the core of the practices of some design practitioners, sensitized to the sensory nature of the world, and the importance of designing body-centered space. An example is Paul Hede, an Australian architect who specializes in designing school spaces that provide emotional support for autistic children. In interview, Hede explained that the qualities of space that autistic kids need include calmness, order and simplicity, minimal materials and detail, the use of natural light, and good acoustics, many of which are usually missing from the environment.[2]

Rather, spaces tend to be constructed with sensory overloads and stimuli that make them hostile for autistic people. In navigating through such spaces, autistic people are prone to withdrawing, seeking to escape the maelstrom of noise, clutter, and busyness. In her autobiography, autistic author Liane Holliday Willey recalls shrinking into a comfort space: "Whenever things became too fuzzy or too loud or too distracting; whenever I began to feel as though I would come unraveled, I knew I could crawl into my alcove and crunch up into it until I felt as square and symmetrical as the alcove itself" (1999, 30). This understanding, of the importance of calmness and repose for autistic people, shapes Hede's work, who designs a multiplicity of school spaces of different shapes, sizes, and colors to give pupils "choices about the amount of connection that they have, so, although they're in an included environment, they can leave it, they can go outside, into other places" (qtd. in Imrie, 2021, 179).

Hede's approaches to spatial relations and place-making highlights the importance of challenging caricatured, ableist conceptions of space, and of acknowledging the multi-sensory nature of the body and the complexities inherent in its interactions with/in space. Such challenges are at the heart of progressive, embodied design practices evident in the work of some past practitioners such as the American architect Frank Lloyd Wright.[3] For Wright, the spatial arrangement of objects was crucial in creating places that "extend the bounds of human individuality" (1936, 187). Practicing from the late-nineteenth to the mid-twentieth centuries, Wright described modern architecture—particularly the dwelling—as anathema to responding to the bodily senses. The dwelling comprised functional spaces described as "boxes"—places often bereft of natural light and inhibiting ease of flow and movement (1936, 177–178). They were, for Wright, without "sense of unity at all nor any sense of space as should belong to a free people" (1936, 177).

The architect's objective was to free people by liberating the body from "dead space" that inhibited human comfort and repose. As Wright observed, nothing less than a revolution in the design of spaces was needed to ensure the "freedom of floor space and elimination of useless heights" (1936, 180). This included dismantling walls and fixtures that prevented the easy flow of bodies, and the dissolution of disconnected spaces so that people could be conjoined with place. The creation of perspective in and of space was paramount to Wright, who primarily used changing levels and elevations to create a sensuous bodily experience of color, light, and movement. Susan Lockhart, an inhabitant of one of his dwellings—the "Solar Hemicycle" house, built in 1936—recalled that it revealed "Wright's understanding that human beings need food for the eye, for the spirit, and a relational scale within structure for a sense of well-being and stimulation" (2003, 14).

Like many designers, Frank Lloyd Wright was involved in a lifelong struggle to liberate the spaces he worked with, or to release them from the normalizing strictures of the building industry. So too for disabled people, in which space is a perennial political issue, and a continuing focal point for contestation over the meaning of citizenship and the rights to be visible and part of the public sphere. The history of disability revolves around disabled people seeking to break out of what Rachel Sara and David Littlefield call the "definitive body," or "the location of the self being contained within a finite space" (2014, 299). Many well-documented social movements of disabled people have challenged illiberal spatial practices related to the finitude of space, and these, by necessity, remain ongoing in a context wherein the nature of a place is fluid and never settled or established. Rather, for disabled people, the politicization of space is a corollary for the making of places in ways that do not reduce the body to a type or a singularity, or render disability irrelevant and invisible.

Notes

1. I met Reiko in Tokyo in July 2014, and she accompanied me in her role as an interpreter to interviews that I was conducting in Japan as part of a European Research Council (ERC) funded project (project number 323777). As a vision-impaired person, she was knowledgeable about navigation and wayfinding issues around Tokyo, and I went with her on walks around the city where she provided me with insights into how a vision-impaired person is able to interact with the environment, and the problems and issues that this entails.
2. I interviewed Paul Hede in October 2015 in Melbourne, Australia as part of my ERC project. He spoke about his work with autistic people, particularly school students, and how he has developed sensitivity and skills in relation to designing for people with a range of different sensory and cognitive impairments. An overview of Paul's ideas and work can be viewed at https://www.hedearchitects.com.au/projects/
3. The material about Frank Lloyd Wright was generated by a British Academy funded project (award reference, SG-101364) that involved two periods of archival research of a collection of Wright's letters and writings lodged in the Getty Research Institute, Los Angeles.

Works Cited

de Certeau, Michel. 1984. *The Practice of Everyday Life*. Berkeley: University of California Press.
Edwards, Claire, and Nicola Maxwell. 2021. "Disability, Hostility and Everyday Geographies of Un/safety." *Social and Cultural Geography* 24 (1): 157–174.
Gieryn, Thomas. 2000. "A Space for Place in Sociology." *Annual Review of Sociology* 26: 463–496.
Hall, Edward. 2019. "A Critical Geography of Disability Hate Crime." *Area* 51 (2): 249–256.
Imrie, Rob. 2021. *Concrete Cities: Why We Need to Build Differently*. Bristol: Bristol University Press.
Imrie, Rob, and Marion Kumar. 1998. "Focusing on Disability and Access in the Built Environment." *Disability and Society* 13 (3): 357–374.
Kafer, Alison. 2013. *Feminist, Queer, Crip*. Bloomington: Indiana University Press.
———. 2017. "Bodies of Nature: The Environmental Politics of Disability." In *Disability Studies and the Environmental Humanities: Toward an Eco-Crip Theory*, ed. Sarah Jaquette Ray and Jay Sibara, 201–242. Lincoln; Univ. of Nebraska Press.
Lockhart, Susan. 2003. "Architecture as Transformational Space." *Frank Lloyd Wright Quarterly* 14 (2): 1–32.
Lynch, Kevin. 1981. *Good City Form*. Cambridge, MA: The MIT Press.
McRuer, Robert. 2002. "Compulsory Able-Bodiedness and Queer/Disabled Existence." In *Disability Studies: Enabling the Humanities*, ed. Brenda Jo Brueggemann, Sharon Snyder, and Rosemary Garland-Thomson, 88–99. New York: MLA Publications.
Merleau-Ponty, Maurice. 1962. *Phenomenology of Perception*. London and New York: Routledge.
Relph, Edward. 1976. *Place and Placelessness*. London: Pion.
Reynolds, Bryan, and Joseph Fitzpatrick. 1999. "The Transversality of Michel De Certeau, Foucault's Panoptic Discourse and the Cartographic Impulse." *Diacritics* 29 (3): 63–80.
Sara, Rachel, and David Littlefield. 2014. "Transgression: Body and Space." *Architecture and Culture* 2 (3): 295–304.
Soja, Edward. 1989. *Postmodern Geographies: The Reassertion of Space in Critical Social Theory*. New York: Verso.
———. 2009. "The City and Spatial Justice." https://www.jssj.org/article/la-ville-et-la-justice-spatiale/?lang=en
Steele, Linda Roslyn. 2021. "Troubling Law's Indefinite Detention: Disability, the Carceral Body and Institutional Injustice." *Social and Legal Studies* 30 (1): 80–103.

Willey, Liane Holliday. 1999. *Pretending to be Normal: Living with Asperger's Syndrome*. London: Jessica Kingsley Publishers.
Withers, Charles. 2009. "Place and the 'Spatial Turn' in Geography and in History." *Journal of the History of Ideas* 70 (4): 637–658.
Wright, Frank Lloyd. 1936. "Organic Architecture." *The Architects Journal* 84: 178–187.

Part I

Into the Wide Open

4

Learning the Camino Real—Disability and the Desert

Sheila Black

The first time I saw the Chihuahuan Desert I wept. It wasn't really the desert, it was the view coming out of the El Paso International Airport, past the now-closed Asarco Chemical plant, which hovers praying mantis-like over the mostly dry Rio Grande and, beyond, the barbed wire and concrete blockades of the border wall as it slopes down into the hills of Juarez. The sky was ethereal blue, the sun white-hot. I had never seen a land so sere or bare. I had moved from Montana sight unseen, and the shock of the brown fields, and the brown-gray slopes of the Franklin Mountains, the huge deserted chemical plant, and the sad cows herded together in bare pens all along 1-10 through Anthony, New Mexico, and on to Las Cruces made me think that I would never be a person who could live in such a place.

I'm sure my reaction had a great deal to do with the fact I was a new mother moving to a strange place with a five-year-old and a six-year-old infant who had just been released from intensive care due to Rh incompatibility after a series of grueling exchange transfusions, which had saved his life the doctors told us "by a miracle," but may have left him with as-yet-to-be-seen problems. Brain damage was common in such cases. In addition, this same child had just been found to have the same disability as I do: X-linked hypophosphatemia (XLH), more commonly known as Vitamin D Resistant Rickets because its

---

S. Black (✉)
The Virginia G. Piper Center for Creative Writing, Arizona State University (ASU), Tempe, AZ, USA
e-mail: sheilafblack@hotmail.com

symptoms resemble those of nutritional rickets—short stature, weak teeth, crooked bones, and a corresponding reduction in mobility.

Mobility was perhaps what I thought of most on that first drive across the broad valley formed by the Rio Grande, a river that, by the time I moved to southern New Mexico, had become so industrialized, so controlled by dams, concrete barriers, border walls, and the like that in many places it barely seemed a river at all—certainly not one to wade or swim in (though, in fact, there is no reason not to). Also, that August, the river, as is often the case, would have been close to completely dry. It is the hottest time, August—after the monsoons of June and July, the one rainy season the Chihuahuan Desert gets—when the heat rises so that the very horizon wavers and each blade of gray-green creosote and mesquite takes on something of the silvered shimmer of insect wings.

I am sure I thought about mobility—or rather my lack of it—for the simple reason that it is almost impossible to move through a real desert without thinking incessantly about survival. Looking out at the wide, hot, bare plains, I couldn't help but wonder, "What if I were stranded out here? Where would I go? What would I do?" Deserts are full of stories of people walking some heroic or terrible journey; the very life of the desert dweller tends to be one that privileges movement. Horses matter in deserts. So do jeeps, trucks, even beater cars, whatever will push you through the land. So does the ability to simply be able to keep marching.

* * *

The highway we were driving followed the very route Juan de Oñate took in 1540, up from El Paso Del Norte or what is now El-Paso-Juarez. The route came to be known as El Camino Real, where the Spanish explorers rose up from Mexico City into the Sierra Norte, winding up just south of Santa Fe.

It can still give a shiver to read the few skeletal accounts that remain. The story of the solider who wept into his hands just south of modern-day Socorro, crying out: "Oh Dios, qué tierra tan solitaria," *Oh God, what a lonely country*. The story of how Oñate and his soldiers ran out of water about an hour south of Las Cruces in what is now San Elizario, Texas. When they finally reached the river, two of their horses drank so much so quickly that their sides burst, and they died.

North from Las Cruces, the route continues across the high plains to Socorro, about two hours by car. This region was named by these same explorers *Jornada del Muerto*, "The Road of Death," or in a more precise translation, "The Single Day's Journey of a Dead Man." Everywhere you turn, there are similar stories—people who walked and did not make it, people stopped in their tracks by the desert.

Even the name Las Cruces reflects this, referring to the fields of wooden crosses erected here and there, commemorating the various travelers who came to grief—some killed by Apache raids or in highway robberies gone wrong; the majority simply perishing through lack of water, resulting in the town's original name: "City of the Garden of Crosses" ("El Pueblo del Jardin de Las Cruces").

* * *

We drove into downtown. It was a Sunday. No one was moving. In some yards, thanks to irrigation, there were green trees—pecans mostly, looking like oasis trees—almost a too-violent green against the rest of the land which was brown and still. The apartment we had rented sight unseen at 1136 Van Patten Avenue—we had come to New Mexico so my husband could attend graduate school at New Mexico State University—proved to be a dark cave-like adobe structure filled with scorpions. The deep windows looked out over a dirt inner courtyard where there were other children with mothers.

In the weeks after, as my husband settled in at his new school, I tried to walk the neighborhood. The heat often defeated me, the stillness, the absence of familiar landmarks. There were few sidewalks. The downtown itself was closed off from traffic but appeared desolate—wide plazas with shuttered structures along both sides. There was a tiny burger place that appeared to be closed, and a bar called The Welcome Inn that looked like it used to be a gas station. Until recently, one of my neighbors told me, you could buy a beer or a margarita through a small window on the street side and drive on down the road.

I never saw anyone at The Welcome Inn—only the low walls of adobe and the sunlight, the sunlight everywhere. 103 degrees. Not like heat in the East, which made it hard to breathe, but a kind of sneaky pitiless heat that you could feel in the back of your skull.

I would stagger a few blocks pushing the stroller and then go to Pioneer Women's Park, founded in 1886 by the Women's Improvement Association, becoming the city's first park. There was a gazebo there where a group of scraggly green herons sometimes seemed to hang out for no reason I could figure, and while my daughter swung herself on the single row of red plastic swings, I'd sit and stare in a panic at the baby, lifting him out of his stroller, trying to decide if he was still desperately sick or getting better.

Although we had been given the "all clear" to make the move with him, he was terribly small and somewhat yellow. Twice a week, because I did not know how to drive, I rode a bus up Picacho Avenue past the mall and then onto the hospital for him to be looked at.

* * *

The third week I was in Las Cruces, one morning as I sat outside the dark, scorpion-filled apartment on a bench in the bright sunlight, the baby suddenly appeared to turn pure white, paper-white—paler than even a white baby should ever appear, so pale I thought at first it must be a trick of the light. I called my husband, who had already started his teaching duties and was at that moment going into a class. He said, "Call a taxi."

I don't remember the taxi ride, though we would have driven, fast I think, the familiar route up Picacho Avenue toward the mall and then cut across Telshor toward the hospital. The clinic had agreed to see me on short notice, but by the time I got there, the baby looked almost normal. The first doctor I saw said I was just paranoid. I was quite a pale person, he said. My baby was pale. I was just anxious because of what we'd already been through with his Rh. I walked out with my daughter holding my hand, my tiny son in my arms. In the parking lot, my daughter and I looked at the baby again. Like a magic trick, a trick of the always-there New Mexico light, he turned ghost-pale again.

* * *

You don't know ahead of time what you will do when disaster descends upon you. What happened to me was I seemed to rise out of my body, to become a kind of fierce floating force. I gripped my daughter's hand, we ran back into the crowded clinic waiting room, and I began to scream. I said, *There is something wrong with my baby*. I said, *I will not leave until you do something*. I saw the doctor I'd just seen behind the counter, and he turned and disappeared down the hall, and another doctor came, a woman this time. And she looked at the baby and she said, "We'll test his blood. Just stop. Sit down. If you are the mother and you think there is something wrong, we'll test his blood just to make sure."

It turned out that, as can sometimes happen with a child who receives multiple transfusions, all his red cells had died off at once. His hematocrit was five, low enough to stop his heart or damage his brain. They gave him another smaller transfusion. They sent us home with liquid iron drops to give him until the anemia resolved.

The liquid iron had a strong cold coin smell that filled the low cave-like apartment. The main thing was he survived. My daughter, the baby, and I returned to our daily walks through the deserted downtown. We walked early in the evening or late at night, for we had learned that afternoon—the time of highest heat and highest sun—was not fit even for children or dogs. In the afternoons, we slept.

* * *

Everything about the desert that I thought I hated changed for me after that. It was as if some kind of filter or veil had been lifted from my eyes, and the things I had feared or distrusted suddenly became familiar and little by little beloved—the huge sky where you could see every movement of cloud; the vertical dark clouds called virga, or "walking rain," because they were rain clouds whose rain somehow never reached earth; the mountains on the far horizon; even the scrubbiness of the town itself. I signed up to take my driver's test. I realized that it was simply not possible to live as I had lived—always afraid to get behind the wheel of a car. I was in the desert now, and this meant I had to be able to move through it in a new way if I expected to stay here.

In the Audubon Society's *Nature Guides: Deserts* (1985), this paragraph appears in the introduction:

> Little rain falls in deserts, usually less than ten inches per year. In some places, such as Death Valley, California, there may be none at all for twelve-month periods. Of equal significance is the unpredictability of precipitation. In fact, the two conditions are related. A worldwide correlation exists between total annual rainfall and the degree to which that rainfall is predictable . . . And it is the combination of the low levels and the unpredictability of the rainfall that makes the environment difficult for many organisms. (28)

Another way to put this is the desert is the very definition of circumstances you can't control and in this is strangely allied with the experience of disability. One reason disability is a site of so much anxiety for the abled is all the ways disability by its very existence seems to challenge many of the more comforting stories about life we tell ourselves—for example, that there is always a cure or a fix for any so-called problem; what is beautiful is closely allied with what is good; the world is not a mystery or a journey but a field that can be plowed and tilled for maximum result.

Unpredictability, inexorability, our helplessness in the face of large fate—these are all experiences people with disability have, and experiences which are made worse by the general fear and suspicion with which many in the abled world view the disabled—we who are in our very bodies evidence of a disruption or subversion of their preferred vision. If you are a person with a disability, you tend to have to adjust to a life of unpredictability. What day will there be pain? Why some days, for no apparent reason, does the pain go away again? Why can you move on this day, but on the next your knee or your hip gives out, and you can only manage a few steps with difficulty? What will it take to survive, and how will you manage this in the most humane way possible? Is there a humane way in a world where you by your very presence are characterized in some unspoken/unspeakable way by the other humans around you as not truly belonging? I came to feel that living in the desert actually suited me, because desert life tends to force similar questions. How does one forge a life in a landscape of such extremes? Who or what actually belongs here?

* * *

When we had lived in Las Cruces for about four years, my family and I bought a house there. This house—though it has been long sold, and longer still since I set foot in it—still occupies my imagination to a remarkable degree. It was an old sprawling adobe surrounded by pecans and juniper, and it backed up onto the *acequia madre,* or "mother canal," which ran through the heart of downtown. The house was scruffy, in a state of considerable disrepair, which was why we were able to afford it. Nevertheless, it had a kind of grandeur—not only the excessively large yard but the way the house itself seemed to have sprung almost organically from the land around it. The original fireplace, or *comal* (now in a windowless room in the center, usually designated as "the library") dated from the 1880s or so, but piece by piece, the house had been added on to—part of it in the 1920s, and the kitchen and laundry room in the 1940s. A brick-floored porch ran along the entire back wall, with a jutting roof supported by huge beams, *vigas,* made of whole trunks of trees. The walls were five feet thick, and because of this, the house stayed cool in the summer, and, even though the street it was on was quite busy, inside one could hear almost nothing of the world beyond. The house felt as if it had been there forever and while most of the improvement projects I began there were doomed to fail—because of my own inertia or the vagaries of the land—I felt in that house as safe and protected as I have ever felt anywhere.

Because of the *acequia*, because we had water rights, I decided to start a garden. This proved much more of a challenge than I expected. The caliche topsoil common in that part of New Mexico was hard as rock most of the year and prevented most plants from even sprouting. You had to buy potting soil and mix it in painstakingly to break down the thick crumbly caliche layer. When you added water, the caliche only became sticky without particularly growing softer and, unless you tended it regularly, every flower bed you made quickly reverted to a hard rock-like crust.

Used to gardening in the East, where just about any seed would sprout, I discovered the tenderness and degree of attention it took to make any living thing in my new home stay alive. Mint, dill, rosemary all bit the dust in my planned herb garden. The basil survived, but only if I remembered to water it multiple times a day. I watered the tomato plants religiously, but they quickly yellowed and withered from lack of iron. At the same time, the land marked everything that did grow with an unusually intense smell and taste. I grew bell peppers from a supermarket seed packet, and they tasted as complicated as chilies, full of deep, rich, bitter heat that seemed to be what the Earth should taste like if it were edible.

We also had a fig tree that bore so much fruit that I came to know many of the birds that shared the space with me—grackles, red-winged blackbirds, the intelligent Chihuahuan desert crows, and the prehistoric-looking roadrunners. I learned what water means, and the history of our *acequia madre*—built in the time when Oñate and the Spaniards used the *acequia* system—built by the labor of the Indigenous peoples they'd enslaved and conquered—to assert control and impose their idea of order on the desert where they hoped to establish a new Spain.

Once or twice a year, the Elephant Butte Water District, which was mysterious and unresponsive to any appeals or normal correspondence, would release water—which you only got by haunting the canal banks and pleading with the ditch riders as they rode through on their golf carts. When water came, my garden—by then so brown-gray and withered it resembled an illustration of Hades in an old children's book—would green and flower overnight. The spadefoot toads which generally remained buried underground would come out in great numbers and sing through the long evenings. The bats that lived in a hole on the backside of the house would slide out like spirits of smoke and scoop the thousands of mosquitoes busy hatching in the standing water. And the pecans, which I always feared had truly died this time around, would race to leaf and flower all in that brief season.

I had never fully known that a place could be hell one week and heaven the next until I occupied that acre of land beside that dusty canal. Every time we hit a dry season, I would tremble at the thought that maybe this year all the trees, all the plants were really dead, that this time we had hit the point of no return.

There was such a point. I know this from the history of our region. Four hours southwest of Las Cruces, in the Gila Wilderness, you can still see the cliff dwellings of the Mogollon people who had established a civilization there from 200-1450 AD. Once, the Mogollon had extended across southwestern New Mexico and Arizona. Their settlements ranged from small valley villages to larger cliff towns and cities. They had vanished beginning in the twelfth century, as had the Anasazi Pueblo peoples to the north, who had built similar cliff cities in northern New Mexico and southern Colorado. In both cases, it is believed that their disappearance came not from war or plague, but simply because of the vagaries of weather.

I found it comforting when I learned that most archeologists do not believe the Mogollon and Anasazi entirely died out, but rather, when the weather became too harsh to sustain their cities or agricultural cultures, they slid back into what archaeologists term "a more prehistoric adaption," becoming nomadic again—transforming themselves back into the hunter gatherers their ancestors had been. I knew, of course, the story could not be that simple, and sometimes when Las Cruces endured as much as one hundred dry days in succession, with not even a single raindrop anywhere, I would try to picture what the Mogollon city dwellers must have felt, waiting and watching the sky, feeling a burst of hope each time the virga cast a shadow over the sun, only to watch whatever rain fell evaporate in mid-air.

* * *

My son did not have brain damage, but he did turn out to have (in addition to XLH) juvenile rheumatoid arthritis (JRA). No one could say why, though I could not help feeling there might be some correlation between his JRA, an immune disorder, and his birth under an autoimmune storm caused by the incompatible Rh factors of his father and me. The JRA began when he was five. One day, he complained his toes hurt; the next he couldn't walk without fits and screams. We took him back to the clinic at Memorial Medical of Las Cruces, and they said they couldn't handle it there. We would have to drive to see a specialist in Albuquerque. By this time, the pain had spread to his hip. Eventually, he would be diagnosed with acute synovitis and held in the hospital for a week. After that, we ended up making the same trip over and over. The pain would always arrive in a different place—his knee, his elbow, his shoulder, and then, almost inevitably, it would spread to the hip joint, where they would have to hospitalize him in case it turned septic.

We became experts in the terminology of his malady—CED rates, referring to the level of immune response; the notion of long-term inflammation; the notion of the pain caused by a sealed joint that undergoes inflammation; the many techniques for pain relief: meditation, special diets, liquid codeine when nothing else worked. It felt, too, as if his illness had pushed us into becoming nomads, pilgrims of a sort—driving the five hours from Las Cruces to Albuquerque, often twice a month, often late at night with a child in severe pain. The long straight line of I-25. Bordered by mountains, crisscrossed by train tracks.

Each time we drove to Albuquerque, we followed the same route Oñate and his soldiers took, the one that filled them with wonder and dread. On these trips, we would stare out at the plains of mesquite, stunted juniper, the occasional cottonwood, often discussing in an almost desultory fashion what we would do if we found ourselves stranded here, exchanging tips, and theories. Go for low ground, that's where the water is. Find a cottonwood. Eat a prickly pear! Talking about the desert in this way helped us manage our dread about what might be going on inside our son or what might be the outcome. Instead, we talked about cactus, how it was myth that you could drink water from a cactus, but if you tied a plastic bag around a cottonwood, its transpiration would give you enough water to stay alive.

Moving haunted me on those journeys. I never drove that route without considering my own body in the world, a body for which even walking at a fairly slow pace was difficult. At the same time, I came to understand that there are ways to move that are not physical alone; sometimes the most important movement you make is in understanding, the ability to grasp where you are in order to see where you have to go.

* * *

If the desert is harsh, it is also an example—like most ecosystems—of the tremendous power of interconnection, of how the smallest decisions and actions can make all the difference. In her desert classic *Land of Little Rain*, Mary Austin describes seeing two mockingbirds circle their nests, frantically flapping their wings for weeks at a time in Death Valley, using their wings as parasols to prevent their eggs from being cooked by the sun. I watched a lot of mockingbirds in Southern New Mexico, hoping to see this behavior in the wild. Although I never did, I had no doubt it was true. It made a desert kind of sense to me—that birds could learn exactly what to do to keep their fledglings alive, even if that meant making parasols of their wings all the long desert summer afternoons.

* * *

My son had crutches for a time. He wore a brace on his wrist. He learned to meditate as a means of managing pain. Because he was nine and a lover of video games, his mantra, to our great amusement, was "guided missile system," which seemed, depending on your viewpoint, paradoxical or sensible. Disability threaded through our house, and we learned to make the necessary adaptions; yet these often—as is the case with most desert living—had consequences. When they were grown up, my daughters laid out in bitter detail that they had hated how our whole household was torqued around the fact of my son's arthritis in addition to his XLH. At the same time, they were grateful, for they had learned so much about what it means to adapt to whatever life might throw at you—a good definition of the knowledge you might need to live in a desert.

Even now, if I close my eyes, I can see the spread of the Jornada del Muerto and the hoodoos that appear as you near Socorro, where you encounter Bosque del Apache, which despite its name is not a forest but a wetlands—a path of water—that sometimes attracts as many as 10,000 sandhill cranes who in their migration over generations have learned to stop there, to get water, to refuel for the next step in the journey. Unlike Oñate's soldiers or the Indigenous people who roamed this land for 20,000 years or more and, at least from what little we know of their mythology, believed it gave them all they needed to thrive, I grew to know the miles mostly as a passenger in a fast-moving car, where vista after vista presented itself and vanished again. I watched the birds and thought of Mary Austin's mockingbirds, and little by little the image of that small tenderness made me see my own disability in a different way. I knew that were I to be abandoned along this road, I would not necessarily survive, because I would not necessarily be able to walk fast enough. But I also knew that even someone strong, someone *abled,* would not necessarily be able to make it either, unless, unless they found a cottonwood to sit under or encountered a sudden summer rain or the chance of a car or horse appearing out of nowhere bearing another desert wanderer.

* * *

4 Learning the Camino Real—Disability and the Desert

On the desert roads of New Mexico, mirages are common. You drive endlessly along dry highways that seem to present lake after glittering lake. This effect is caused by the abrupt meeting of the hot desert earth with the cooler desert air which bends the light, and this radical disparity of temperature is, of course, caused by lack of water. The hot air that radiates just above the ground torques the light so that it reflects only sky, making it appear as if you are looking into water.

One thing most people like about deserts is that even their fabled heat does not linger. Unlike the muggy warmth of the East and the Midwest, deserts cool rapidly at night and, even in peak times, desert heat is generally not as uncomfortable as humid heat, though it is more lethal.

Again from the Audubon's *Nature Guides: Deserts*:

> Although high evaporation rates are good for your personal comfort, they can be a problem for the resident plants and animals which must replace the water lost. Remarkably, evaporation in the American deserts ranges from seventy to 160 inches per year. Moreover, most desert sites receive only four to eight inches of precipitation a year. Thus the disparity between precipitation and evaporation is enormous. (1985, 32)

I read this to say that if there's any life in the desert, it's a kind of miracle. It further illustrates the pointed mysteriousness of all our life stories. We do not know where we are going; we know life is rare and in many ways an anomaly. We know it persists, though we cannot say for sure why.

* * *

The first day in Las Cruces, we checked into our apartment and went walking through the neighborhood. No one but us appeared to be moving, and we could feel the dryness inside spreading until our heads ached. I was not used back then to the effects of dry heat. When I got back to our apartment, I felt dizzy, breathless, and a neighbor child (her name was Maya, and she was six years old) ran out with a plastic cup of water. Then she showed me something she liked to do. She poured some water on the hood of our car and said, "Watch." And the water quickly, irrevocably, simply vanished, as if the air itself was eating it up. We should have been horrified, but instead we were entranced. We did it again, and again, as if it were the oldest magic, the land itself speaking to us, a kind of giant invisible cat lapping up whatever we put in front of it, saying, "I am here, and I know you are, too."

Deserts are ravenous, deserts are rapacious, deserts are places where it is perilously easy to lose yourself. Deserts are not easy. Similarly, disability is not easy or comfortable for most people. Much as the desert is usually described as a place of exile, a place of suffering, the place before whatever oasis you wish to get to, historically disability has been conceived of as an anomaly—a condition, put most crudely, that *should not exist*, that should somehow be fixed—cured or eradicated. Yet as a person with a disability, to have a body like mine, or my son's, has been, despite its challenges, the source of so much wonder and discovery. Similarly, to be a desert dweller is to be in the position of always being reminded by the land itself that you are not the center of anything—you are part of a larger canvas in which your human concerns are hardly the paramount issue. The story of water is much more, or the story of rock, or the story of juniper, creosote, and rabbit brush. In the desert, you can see the elements collide and breathe in something of the long song of long time. If deserts are pitiless, they are also, for the same reason, forgiving. Similarly, disability offers the opportunity to view human order from the margins—to learn from that liminal space what matters and what is more or less irrelevant, how very many ways there are of moving through time and space.

Work Cited

Macmahon, James. 1985. *The Audubon Society Nature Guides: Deserts*. A Chanticleer Press edition. New York: Alfred A. Knopf.

5

Headlamps and Fireside Light

Rachel Kolb

For several years now, I've owned a Petzl outdoor headlamp whose strap is emblazoned with the phrase ACCESS THE INACCESSIBLE ®. I bought this headlamp at my local REI without seeing the slogan, took it home, lifted it out of the box, and chuckled out loud. On my next camping trip, I pulled the headlamp from my pack and waved it in front of a close friend's eyes. Her mouth fell open when she saw the message on the strap, and she cried out, "Time for accessibility!" I didn't have to explain to my hearing friend why I found Petzl's unintentional deaf-marketing strategy so funny—she got it immediately.

I snapped the headlamp around my skull, flipped on the gleaming white light, and aimed it straight at her face. "I'm claiming my right to access," I said. "Trademarked."

Petzl was on to something. As the woods around us dimmed with the advancing night, my friend's face darkened and her signed words vanished. But as soon as I clicked on my headlamp—*Lo!* We found our way back to each other.

Dark nights outdoors can still conjure memories of campfire gatherings in hearing friends' backyards, where I arrived to find shadowy faces and bodies sprawled against the fire's orange glow, volleying loose remarks through the air, most of which flew off like dying sparks before my eyes. They make me recall one group camping trip I joined in college, where nearly no one signed,

---

R. Kolb (✉)
Harvard Society of Fellows, Cambridge, MA, USA
e-mail: rachel.r.kolb@gmail.com

© The Author(s), under exclusive license to Springer Nature Switzerland AG 2024
S. B. Mintz, G. Fraser (eds.), *Placing Disability*, Literary Disability Studies,
https://doi.org/10.1007/978-3-031-41219-6_5

where the fireside chatter grew until I excused myself early and went to lie in the tent. Call such conversations inaccessible—because they are. They have been for deaf people long before me. As the deaf wilderness explorer William Swett wrote after spending a night outdoors with a hearing companion back in the 1860s, "The darkness put it out of our power to converse, which was rather uncomfortable" (1874, 22).

But not always. *The woods are lovely, dark and deep.* Maybe for my non-signing hearing friends, such woodsy loveliness springs from the sonic intimacy of dim fireside talks, not unlike those particularly hearing comforts of late-night restaurant dinners with the waiters darting between tables, turning the wall-switches lower and lower. My body will never understand the appeal of sitting apart and speaking to each other in the dark, like a bunch of isolated cartoon-speech bubbles, but the night still has its loveliness to offer.

On a recent camping trip, with deaf friends this time, I discovered that one of them had the same Petzl headlamp. "You ever look at the slogan on that light of yours?" I asked her wryly in American Sign Language (ASL).

She frowned and turned over the strap. Then her face lit up. "Accessibility!" She waved to the group, and all of us laughed knowingly. "I don't know how I never noticed it," she said.

Before our all-signing camping trip, this deaf friend had sent an email to the group matter-of-factly reminding us to bring as many headlamps and LED lights as possible, for obvious nighttime hangout reasons. We showed up at the campsite with our bags full of assorted flashlights, lanterns, and other lighting options. As the autumn night advanced and the shadows grew, some alarm went off inside us: time to put up the lights. Our conversations stopped abruptly. We stood up, burrowed into our hoard of light, stretched ropes between trees, hung lanterns, checked in with each other: "Can you see now? That better? Okay, awesome." Then we settled down, gathered closer, fiddled with our headlamps, made amused faces at our lighting optimization. We piled logs and sticks by the campfire, told more stories, coaxed the flames higher.

Deaf people are like moths, one old deaf joke goes. I never feel more like a cozy brown moth than when I urge a campfire to peak rolling yellow flame and turn to a signing friend in its glow. When our bodies gather like this, darkness is no longer a curtain that divides but a backdrop for shared pinpricks of light. One could say the woods become *accessible* through our efforts, our lighting, our attention to visual communication—yet sitting outdoors, both in solitude and in the company of others, can feel like something different altogether. Here, my butt perched on a log, my headlamp dispelling the darkness or switched off in my pocket, I become more acutely aware of how my body interacts with the world around me. The wilderness, for all its longstanding mythologies about self-discovery through the prism of nature, can invite me to gaze through a different prism—one that uncovers my foundational rules of existence, by which I simply mean the physical textures I encounter through different gradients of light and dark and movement and breath. As I sit within a forest that our language can still describe as remote or inaccessible, I ponder the things our bodies can know. I ponder how the mountain itself shapes this knowledge, of ourselves and each other and the frontiers around and between us.

* * *

The first time I went camping with the hearing friend I've mentioned, we didn't know each other very well. She was just starting to learn ASL. We tried out different conversation patterns as we loaded up our packs and trekked through the Georgia woods into North Carolina. I posed for a goofy photo as I stepped across the state line for the first time, my thumbs up and knees splayed. As would become our habit, I started hiking behind my friend while audibly announcing extemporaneous trail observations with my deaf voice, reading her signs, and fingerspelling from the backside as she responded. We found that, by configuring our bodies this way, we could carry on a roving trail conversation for hours.

That first night at the campsite, it poured. As we stood beside the creek pumping water, my raincoat hood jammed up around my ears, I revealed to my friend how deeply inscribed my mother's childhood warnings still are within me: "Be careful, your hearing aids!" I ripped the electronics from my head and ushered them to safety, tightly wrapped in a plastic bag in the tent. In my world, being drenched means being deaf. Sound and water do not—cannot—mix.

Darkness fell, transforming the landscape. My friend and I discovered each other's preferences for arranging gear, prepping food, setting up the tent. We put up the lights. I saw her recognize this as important. We made eye contact, pulled out the flashlights, figured out how close we needed to huddle together under a tarp in our rain jackets. Too early in our friendship for the jokes about *accessing the inaccessible.* Those would come later, once these outdoor rituals became familiar. Not too early, though, for sharing stories about past camping trips with our families, about how we'd first learned the joys of mud and rain and being dirty outside.

No fire that night. Too rainy. We staked out our single dry spot beneath the tarp, cooked some food on the camp stove, just the two of us in the wet and the pitch-black. Soon we saw that we'd brought too many provisions. We'd have to stash our leftovers with the rest of our food before bed. We started to discuss logistics.

"What about bears?" my friend said, signing in the too-white light from the flashlight. Her face was ghostly.

I shrugged. It wasn't that we had come unprepared. We'd brought a bear canister. We knew to stow it in the woods, to contain our food far away from the tent. In my mind, this was straightforward: be smart, clean up, leave the campsite in order, go to bed. Nothing more to do. But I had things to learn about how dark woodsy nights sometimes felt for my hearing friends.

"If a bear comes, I want to hear it," my friend said. She was already gazing out into the rain and the dark woods, her head pivoting. "I'm going to set up some of our dishes over there."

"Why?" I said.

"If a bear comes, they'll clatter and make noise."

For all my past camping trips with my hearing family, I'd rarely thought about the phenomenon of hearing wildlife at night. "What would you do if you *did* hear a bear?"

"Probably nothing," my friend admitted. "Lie in the tent. Listen. But at least I'd know. And the clatter could scare the bear away."

I do not remember what I said as I helped clean our dishes and got ready to dive out of the damp and into my sleeping bag. Probably something like "Have fun with that!"

The next morning, the dishes were intact in their pile across the campsite. The bear-can lay undisturbed near the roots of a tree. We'd put our food away appropriately. No bear had come to visit. I asked my friend if she'd heard anything during the night, and she remarked that the rain had been very loud, pounding on the fly of the tent as the wind lashed at the guy lines. This, I realized, was part of why she'd been worried about hearing (or not hearing) potential intruders. I had heard nothing, of course.

"It must be so hard to be hearing," I grinned at my friend. This was perhaps the first time I made this joke to her, but it wouldn't be the last. In the years to follow, we'd become familiar with the ways we each experienced the mountains along the East Coast, from Georgia to Virginia to New Hampshire. We became used to each other's typical hiking pace, cadence, rhythm, energy, appetite. We learned that we had a similar desire for the mountain and the focus the trail could give, and we discussed what this desire even meant, what the mountain meant for our understandings of self and achievement. And we examined what our different sensory experiences meant, too. We chuckled about sounds—sounds that she heard and I did not. Like the many camping trips where she lay awake in the tent listening to thunder and torrential rain; or the night at a campground where our neighbors revved their sportscars up and down the gravel road for hours; or the time she actually did hear a bear rummaging through some poorly stored garbage at a nearby campsite.

"There was really a bear this time?" I exclaimed the following morning.

"Yes!" she said, repeating herself for emphasis. "There was a bear! And I couldn't even tell you!"

"Well, you could have."

"But that would have involved turning on the light! The bear would have seen!"

"You could still have shaken me awake."

Then we both laughed, suddenly arrested by the image of ourselves just inches apart in a tiny tent, one happily asleep and the other braced awake, listening to a bear make a racket before getting bored and lumbering off.

"I wouldn't trade places with you," I jibed.

"Don't I know it," she said.

I later told the bear story to a non-signing hearing acquaintance who asked me how my camping trip had gone.

"That's so scary!" my acquaintance said, missing my raised eyebrows and snicker. "Weren't you afraid about not hearing it?"

But when I told the story to deaf friends, they laughed with me. Then they chimed in with their own stories of sound and the woods, of outings with friends both deaf and hearing, variations of old ASL tales about deaf hunters and lions and lumberjacks and the things they hear and see in the wilderness—or don't. *Funny in deaf, not in hearing.*

Other signing hearing friends, including some ASL interpreters, have also shared in the sonic humor about bears and owls and mice and all the creatures I can imagine but cannot see or hear in the dark. "I apologize for my overly sensitive hearing ears," one interpreter friend laughed as she and I sat by the fire on our own car camping trip. We'd optimized the lighting as usual, gathered near each other in the night. I'd already noticed her glancing around, her ears registering noises that she'd hardly bothered with before dusk.

When it is dark, when it is raining, when we find ourselves tired in unfamiliar places, these woods have many things to reveal in us.

Swish! I see a hearing friend jump. "What was that?"

Brrrrk. "I think I heard—I don't even know. Oh, it's okay."

Gromp!

Thonk!

Poor hearing people. The darkness sometimes brings them into contact with their primal instincts. The deaf members of the group shrug. The things that go bump in the night do not scare us.

* * *

Why do I make light of hearing (or not hearing) bears in the woods? Why doesn't it bother me not to hear that thunderstorm rolling in, or the sounds outside the tent at night? Sometimes, when I mention hiking and camping trips to hearing acquaintances, they express unease about the dangers of the wilderness. I notice that they often frame danger in sonic terms. They imply that hearing is essential for outdoor safety, even outdoor competence. Such responses aren't far removed from the unease some hearing acquaintances still express to me when I mention how I love to drive my car. (How do deaf people even drive? Hike? Go anywhere by themselves?). Far easier for a deaf person to stay home, I gather, than to venture out where there may be bears, wildlife, thunder and lightning and unexpected weather, slippery rocks and ice, forest fires, natural disasters, hunters, other human beings. What if I get lost, get in trouble, don't hear something approaching, can't call for help? In these terms, being safe—and competent—must mean being hearing.

Being outdoors, in remote and inaccessible woods, seemingly requires all of one's body and mind and strength. We remain haunted by the ghosts of tough, bearded frontiersmen with their preternatural sensory gifts. Yet when I pack up and drive off to a National Forest Service campground, even when I hike up to some more distant backcountry sites, I am not quite out on the frontier. Surely, these places require wilderness knowledge. And surely, there are circumstances in which sound might be more essential—while out on a search and rescue mission, for instance. But I also feel comfortable in my body as it is. I know other ways to observe, which for me also means honoring how this body operates. I have never been hearing, so why would I fret after the sounds of bears and snapping twigs and rumbling thunder? My flesh has other rules to follow.

When I camped and hiked as a child, I learned that spending time in the mountains requires good common sense. This was what my father always said to me: "Just use your common sense." The way he described it, mountain common sense didn't boil down to a single sense. It meant bringing maps and appropriate clothing and enough food and water, especially in the arid regions of New Mexico where I grew up. It meant checking the weather forecast and watching the sky, feeling the direction of the wind and smelling the air for rain. It meant going out with a plan, with other people, with an understanding of yourself and your limits. It meant stopping, resting, sometimes turning around. It meant paying attention.

"Which way is north?" my father would say to me when I was young, looking up at the slant of light through the Ponderosa pines. I'd point wildly in all directions, but he always seemed to know the answer. "It's that way," he'd say.

And so I learned to notice how the sun moved across the landscape, to gauge when the shadows were getting short or long, to register when my legs were getting tired, to anticipate an incoming storm at high elevation. Surely, my father brought his own ideas about physical strength and conquest to those wilderness outings. I know he did, and surely, I have inherited some of these from him. Plenty of photos still exist of me at the summit of one peak or another, grinning, my arms stretched out in lofty achievement. Doubtless it is from my father that I wound up with my own set of pesky frontiersman ideals, my own desires about fitness and ability and climbing the mountain—at the very least, as the route toward a darned good view. But from my father and others in my family, I also learned to claim these woods as mine.

When my family went camping during my childhood, I became familiar with clambering up the rocks on the dry New Mexico trails, and with taking my hearing aids out before plunging into streams. I found rhythm in the pulse of my legs, learned to look back to make sure everyone stayed together. I made stick forts in the woods after letting my parents know where they could find me. I also went to deaf camp in Colorado. There, we signed outdoor songs, sat around the campfire and watched each other share ASL stories in the glow. We went on zipline outings, took overnight backpacking trips, and braved whitewater rafting adventures—always prefaced by the shared ritual of leaving our hearing aids on the bus. We tapped each other's shoulders and shouted in our deaf voices and learned how to shake our flashlights at someone so they would turn around and look. All these outdoor conversations took place in sign. Sometimes, one of the staff members was hearing and would let us know what she heard in the distance, or would interpret what the rafting guide said, but this sharing of knowledge felt like part of being outdoors with other people. The hearing staff members often didn't bother with sharing ambient sounds, anyway. These weren't important.

When we imagine the wilderness as a space of honed or sharpened senses—of eagle-eye vision or the deer's swiveling ears—we sometimes ignore the interdependence between hiking friends and how they can laugh and bumble along together. And when our inherited mountain-language veers toward speed, strength, acuity, survival, conquest, achievement, it becomes too easy to write an essay on deafness and the outdoors and fall deep into a particular gully. That is, it becomes too easy to claim deaf visual sharpness, sensory gifts, physical strength, or collective understanding as the basis of a new communion with nature. To claim that old and ongoing mantra: *Deaf can!* Or to toss out that recurring phrase, which I myself used to say: *Deaf people can do anything except hear.*

I learned both of these mantras when I went to deaf camp, with my staticky blonde bangs and oversized T-shirts. It was a gift to me then, and in many ways still is, to realize the resourcefulness I and others had for getting out into the mountains with their fresh air and wildflowers. I knew that sometimes the hearing people in the town of Aspen saw us deaf summer campers as novelties, such as when we participated in the annual Fourth of July parade and wound up in the local newspaper, but I'd long since sensed that this could be the hearing response to seeing deaf people do, well, pretty much anything. My childhood scrapbook is filled with various news clippings I appeared in as a kid, by virtue of being deaf and nothing else. These blurbs included, but were not limited to, outdoor pursuits: skiing, exploring the Rio Grande River, helping break ground for a new deaf-preschool campus. (The latter might not technically be outdoorsy, but I *was* outside, holding a shovel.)

Is this what it originally meant for me to gain access to the inaccessible? Maybe. Picking up some outdoor activities like skiing did require certain measures of access, such as looping my father into a weekend adaptive ski and snowboard program as my "interpreter." I now wonder if highlighting deaf people for outdoor participation draws attention to some presumed inaccessibility in nature itself, furthering more grand stories of overcoming. As Eli Clare observes (2015), ableism is tangled up with the stories we tell about these mountains and the feats they require.

Gaining access to that inaccessible frontier, climbing summits with my physical strength, observing natural details with my preternatural deaf vision: these are among the stories I could write about the woods, to satisfy these latent expectations for mastery. And this is also where the language of access sometimes feels incomplete. As John Lee Clark (2021) puts it, the notion of access can assume that there is only one world. It is a world to strive after, to try and be included by. It implies obstacles to be cleared, fixed points to climb, rather than what I sometimes see—a proliferation of different routes meandering off in various directions. We can trek along these disparate routes even when we are right beside each other.

My National Parks Service (NPS) access pass is one of my favorite possessions. I flash it every time I drive up to a park gate, though I have sometimes considered whether I look "disabled enough" to use it. The pass features a wheelchair, the universal symbol of disability. I may be a wheelchair user at some point later in my life, due to circumstances I do not yet anticipate, in which case I hope to take advantage of the growing network of paved accessible trails in scenic places. But right now, I am not. I experience deafness as a disability requiring accommodation, yet I also experience it as a linguistic difference and as a cultural ethos. This sometimes unstable blend means that access isn't just ASL-interpreted ranger tours and captioned visitor center videos. It also springs from the people I meet and hike and chat with, from the ways we understand each other in the places we inhabit. At this point, aren't we talking less about access than about some more deeply human sensibility? About the fluidity and insight it takes to live more communally?

I wonder, then, what exactly this NPS access pass suggests about disability and formal recompense, about barriers to the woods and who belongs. I know my own barriers to entry were very low. A signing family with resources and knowledge, a childhood spent in the Rocky Mountains, nearby deaf-friendly camps and outings: these are among the reasons I claim the wilderness as mine. Other people without diagnosable impairments experience greater barriers to these mountains than I do, for reasons social and cultural and economic. What work does my access pass do? Is it recognizing and providing reparations for my "permanent disability," as somehow more significant than these? Is it compensating for all the ways that forests and trails and spoken-language parks programming are still not ADA-accessible? Or boosting the opportunity I *do* have to experience the parks, even given the "substantial limitations" I face in "major life activities," which presumably include hearing all those babbling brooks and chirping songbirds?

Whatever the rhetorical function of my pass, whatever it says about disability and individual access and compensation, it has saved me hundreds of dollars. It has also turned me into an enviable weekend outdoors companion: eager to hit the trails given reasonable weather, with free camping and free park-entry perks besides. In our modern vocabulary of credentials and paperwork and bureaucracy, this must be one logical consequence of all those flat-lined audiograms and visits to the audiologist's testing booth. I have achieved VIP status in these wilderness places for life. Which sometimes amuses me, because there is one last feature of these wild and remote places that lurks in the collective cultural imagination: their silence.

* * *

Supposedly, I experience silence in the woods, during those moments when my hearing companions lie awake listening to owls or rumbling thunder or revved-up cars. Or when we stand and survey those roaring waterfalls or babbling brooks. These notions about silence are partly true. When I wake up in the tent in the middle of the night, I don't hear anything. I am sometimes annoyed that I don't know if it is raining or not. I am pleased that the pit-pattering sound hasn't kept me awake, but what if I need to pee? I want to predict whether peeing outside will be a quick and painless task, or whether it will involve an unpleasant drenching. I reach my hand up to the flap of the tent in the dark and feel for the rhythm of raindrops. Soft and gentle, it feels like making contact with something elemental.

But what I experience in the outdoors and in other secluded places isn't silence as much as the inner space for thoughts to expand. It's physical rhythm and cadence. It's the solace of exhaling breath. Sometimes, when I wear my hearing aid and cochlear implant, my sensory experience does involve some sound. I have stepped down the trail to hear someone calling my name from behind, then spun wildly around to see what's happening. A few times, with deaf hiker friends, we've laughed hard at our sporadic reactions to on-the-trail shouting. ("Wow, good listening skills!" we'll say. Or: "Oh, well. That didn't work.") Sound sometimes informs our knowledge of these woods, but it is usually secondary. It is idiosyncratic, weird, unreliable. It doesn't give this rich world its depth and dimension.

Yet silence, as much as those assorted hearing acquaintances seem to associate it with insensibility or danger, also has its own odd cultural cachet. "I'm looking forward to getting away to some peace and quiet," someone will say to me about their upcoming mountain getaway. "I need some silence to hear myself think." Or I read articles about noise pollution, about how our state and national parks are louder than ever because of human-created hubbub and machinery. I learn about how this affects wildlife habitat and migration. As with light pollution from cities, true silence is becoming harder to find. It is something elusive, vaunted, rare. It has become a sort of luxury.

I know pristine and uninterrupted silence, whatever that means, very well. And I also do not know it at all. I can create and access silence whenever I want without a special pass, as I joke with hearing friends, and it is also far from any vocabulary I understand. These laden sensory terms and values, of sound and silence and whatever it means to gain access to them, do influence my understanding of the mountain. How could they not? They are everywhere in our language and in our shared frontier mythologies. But they also do not quite capture my own sensations of existence, of what Thoreau called "the essential facts of life" (2008, 65). When I think of the woods, I am more likely to think of sight, light, golden rays illuminating the veins of leaves, shared glances, the hard scuffing of a boot across a tree root, the magic when my foot knows just how to amble up a rock, warm hands tapping my shoulder when the fire dims at night, the crispness of the tent zipper cinching shut. The brook need not babble; it already says enough through its silvery cascades. I find it a mystery to describe anything I perceive, almost as much of a mystery as imagining the sensations of someone else's experiences.

I have hiked along, sometimes for hours, with a friend or family member and found myself as thoroughly in my body as I imagine they were in theirs. This can be the gift of the trail: of being in your body, the body you have on that incline and in that moment. Yours is not always the body you wish you had, the body you wish already stood at the grand summit or lounged back at the campsite sipping a post-hike beer, but it still does what it does. It still tells you what it knows. Once, several years ago, when out with that close hearing friend, my body told me that we'd just had a magnificent hike. The temperature was cool but not too cold. I'd been watching the late winter light through the browned leaves along the trail. My legs churned and my thoughts roved as they only do when I am on foot. It felt silent and, aside from my grunting breath, completely still.

"It feels so beautiful and quiet out here right now," I said.

My friend grinned at me, not in a way that diminished my experience, but in genuine surprise and amusement.

"I've been hearing chainsaws over there for the last hour," she said. "It's so annoying."

"Oh, really," I said dryly. Then I laughed. How many times had we shared a moment like this, when I felt terrific and she felt terrible, or when her pack was loaded and ready to go, but I was wallowing in how awfully hungry I felt? When I noticed something new and told her, or the other way around? Our rhythms often did align, but our bodies were still slippery. Our thoughts plunged in different directions. They couldn't be pinned down. These are the things that always, perhaps, remain inaccessible. How could they ever be otherwise?

"Yes," my friend said. "I can also hear a highway off in the distance right now. And cars. I wish these woods were silent."

"I hope you've enjoyed listening to all that," I said, before both of us continued onwards together. "It sounds so nice."

Works Cited

Clare, Eli. 2015. *Exile and Pride: Disability, Queerness, and Liberation*. Durham, NC: Duke University Press.

Clark, John Lee. 2021. "Against Access." *McSweeney's 64: The Audio Issue*. https://audio.mcsweeneys.net/transcripts/against_access.html

Swett, William. 1874. *Adventures of a Deaf-Mute*. Boston: Boston Deaf-Mutes' Mission.

Thoreau, Henry David. 2008. *Walden*. New York: Norton.

6

A Sense of Place & Cyberspace: The Hybrid Way I Live, Work, and Play

Gyasi Burks-Abbott

It was a stormy night in October 2019, and I was home alone in my apartment in Bedford, Massachusetts. I had spent the day working in my cubicle at the Institute for Community Inclusion at UMass Boston before going to Harvard Square to meet with a colleague and friend for an informal chat. The trip to Harvard Square was a detour from my usual commute between Boston and Bedford. Fortunately, the friend I was meeting had introduced me to the transit app a few weeks earlier, and when I downloaded it onto my phone, I'd added another tool to my high-tech Swiss Army knife which already included Google Maps and the Uber app. I now had everything I needed to get around despite my poor sense of direction and my inability to drive.

After my brief meeting in Harvard Square, I got home just in time to beat the big storm that slammed into Bedford, cutting off all electricity—leaving me both literally and figuratively in the dark. No lights, no internet, no TV, and certainly no way I was going to make the conference I was scheduled to attend the next day. And to think that this conference was on technology, and I was going to miss it because of a complete failure of technology. Here I was completely cut off from the rest of society like a hermit living off the grid.

G. Burks-Abbott (✉)
Leadership Education in Neurodevelopmental and Related Disabilities (LEND) Program at Boston Children's Hospital and the UMass Boston Institute for Community Inclusion, Boston, MA, USA
e-mail: burks1900@yahoo.com

But then I remembered that my cell phone was fully charged. With just a toggle to the right to turn on data mode, I had full access to the internet and social media. I received e-mail updates from my energy company, and I was kept company by my neighbors and friends on Facebook. I may have been marooned on my own little island, but I didn't feel isolated or even alone. I felt connected to others caught in the same storm. It was a sign of things to come. Not six months later, nature would once again assert its power, this time on a global scale in the form of a virus, shutting everything down. And the only means people would have to stay connected would be computer technology.

The storm subsided, my electricity was restored, and I attended the conference the next day. I don't remember if I got any sleep, but the adrenaline rush and a few cups of coffee kept me going. Called "Talking Tech 2019," the conference was organized by the Association of Developmental Disabilities Providers, a trade organization in Massachusetts, and the state's Department of Developmental Services. As stated on the conference website, the purpose of the event was to "celebrate the promise of technology for [the] empowerment and social inclusion of individuals with disabilities." To that end, technology gurus discussed the myriad ways different high-tech devices could be marshaled to help people with disabilities live independently in their own homes.

During the pandemic, the ability of people with disabilities to live in their own homes would be about more than just "empowerment and social inclusion." It would have life-and-death consequences. As institutional settings experienced the rapid spread of COVID-19, they became dangerous, and as the National Council on Disability (NCD) noted, "sheltering in place" for people in congregate settings often meant "dying in place."

The NCD issued a report (*Strengthening the HCBS Ecosystem: Responding to Dangers of Congregate Settings during COVID-19*, 2022) assessing the impact of the pandemic on people with disabilities. The council recommended increased government investment in Home and Community Based Services (HCBS), stating that this was not a new issue, just one that had become more pressing:

> The pandemic has shone a light on our nation's insufficient investment in Home and Community Based Services. These services are a life-line for millions of people with disabilities who desire to live independently in their respective communities . . . COVID-19 disproportionality effected people with disabilities, both young and old, who lived in congregate settings, and at 20 percent of the 1 million deaths, they bore the brunt of the pandemic. (1, 8)

But even without the understanding that would later come about the perils of congregate living, the message of the technology conference still resonated with me. As I listened to presentations about smart homes and appliances, remote monitoring devices, telehealth, and cybersecurity, I reflected on my own experience with a cell phone during a blackout the night before.

Technology designed specifically for disabled people is called *assistive technology*, a nomenclature I never questioned until challenged at a conference some years ago by a speaker with physical disabilities. I wasn't challenged directly; I was in the audience when the speaker asked, "Has anyone here ever used an elevator?" After we all indicated "yes," she said, "Congratulations. You've all used assistive technology." I'd never thought of it that way, but my mind ran with it. Able-bodied or not, we're all mortal—not simply because we die but because there's only so much our physical brains and bodies can do while we live. We all rely on technology to overcome limitations. Why should there be a stigma attached when a disabled person does it?

During the pandemic, there was a great deal of resistance to the technology of the face mask. While much of it was driven by partisan politics, there was also the fact that many people refused to accept their vulnerability to disease. They'd brag about the robustness of their immune systems and point out that most of the people being hospitalized and dying from COVID were old or already in poor health. They'd cloak their objections in arguments about choice and freedom. But what of the rules they were willing to follow? Removing shoes and belt at a TSA security check point? Fine. Wearing a mask on the plane? That signifier of sickness? No way.

Incidentally, the technology that assisted me in my daily life was mainstream and didn't carry the stigma of being associated mainly with disability. In addition to the apps on my phone, there was online banking and shopping as well as automatic bill paying. And to keep myself socially engaged despite my introversion (on top of my autism) and the fact that I lived alone, there was social media—especially Facebook—which I have accessed for years.

The internet was made for someone like me who is terrible at keeping in touch through letter writing. In fact, one of my oldest friends is a woman I went to community college with over thirty years ago. When I moved out of the state to attend a four-year college, this friend kept our connection alive by always including me in her e-mail blasts. Now she is a Facebook friend along with people I've known at different stages of my life going back to infancy. Yes, infancy. A woman who babysat me when I was five months old friended me a few years ago. I didn't remember her, but my mother did.

In addition to keeping me connected and engaged, social media also facilitated my self-expression. I have always been told I have a way with words—neuropsychological testing consistently reveals a verbal ability that's off the charts (while my visual-spatial skills barely register). That doesn't mean, however, that I'm always able to communicate, particularly in the back-and-forth of normal conversation. I get tongue-tied and forget what I wanted to say, or I think of the perfect reply long after the moment has passed. An interaction on Facebook is like a conversation in slow-motion that gives me more time to process and reflect. Indeed, my "immediate" response to a post or a comment can come a day or two later without making me seem out-of-sync.

For the most part, I enjoy the time I spend in the virtual public square. It's a great "place" to gather and discuss important issues or just to shoot the breeze and share some memes. Unfortunately, this amicable and civil discourse that's fit for a parlor room or salon can often devolve into a barroom brawl. I think part of the problem is that people forget that just because you can post anything at any time doesn't mean you should.

I sometimes perform a thought experiment where I place myself in the late nineteenth or early twentieth century. I imagine all the steps I'd need to go through if I wanted to express some random thought. I'd have to write a letter and mail it or visit the telegraph office to send a telegram. Maybe if I were lucky, I'd convince a newspaper editor to publish me. With all this effort, I bet this earlier version of me would really have to consider whether it was worth it.

Of course, this analogy to a hypothetical me living in an earlier era is not perfect. The actual me living in this era posts many things that I'd never bother with if I couldn't do so from the comfort of my own home (often in my pajamas). However, before I post I do try to exercise a high level of critical thought. Is this as funny as I think it is, or even interesting? Could this inadvertently cause offense? I try to be just as circumspect as a consumer of content—thinking with equal critical awareness about what I read and write online and off.

At the turn of the twenty-first century, I was earning my master's in Library and Information Science at Simmons University in Boston. I remember how many of my professors viewed the internet and the World Wide Web almost as existential threats. If everyone can swiftly acquire information online, who needs librarians anymore? But the concern was more than just a worry about professional obsolescence; there was a genuine fear of this vast and unregulated information landscape. On the one hand, the net was something to be celebrated. It was the democratization of information where anyone with an internet connection could create content and have it widely distributed. On the other hand, the lack of rules and standards meant that there was no way of weeding out bad information. Indeed, instead of becoming obsolete, librarians would be needed now more than ever: to teach information literacy, the technical term for assessing and evaluating online sources. It's the antidote for the viral spread of misinformation.

After the pandemic hit, the internet became the ultimate safe space despite its many perils and dangers. Remote work, once an accommodation disabled employees had to fight for, was now standard business practice. Incidentally, I was already working semi-remotely when the pandemic hit. I was completing a fellowship designated for a disabled person at UMass Boston's Institute for Community Inclusion (ICI). I only had to spend twenty hours a week in the office, which enabled me to do most of my work from home. ICI itself had already adopted a hybrid model. Some ICI employees live outside of Massachusetts, so staff meetings would be held in person, with people logging in remotely via Zoom.

In February 2020, I was preparing for my March trip to Washington, D.C to attend the annual Disability Policy Seminar (DPS) and to speak to legislators on Capitol Hill. The DPS is put on each year by the Association of University Centers on Disabilities (AUCD), a national network of university- and hospital-affiliated disability programs. The seminar offers an opportunity to interact with colleagues from across the country, to learn about the latest happenings in public policy and research, and to educate lawmakers about disability priorities. I had attended the year before for the first time and was looking forward to participating again.

Then the pandemic struck. The trip to D.C. was cancelled but not the DPS. AUCD created a virtual platform for the conference. My colleagues and I were able to listen to live presentations and even interact with other attendees, just as we would have in person. The visits to Capitol Hill were cancelled but not the meetings with senators and representatives. We met over Zoom and had face-to-face conversations. We discussed issues that had long been important to the disability community but were now exacerbated by the pandemic. For instance, recipients of Supplemental Security Income (SSI) could not have more than $2,000 worth of assets in their checking accounts, which had posed a problem to me personally in the past. I was often caught in the dilemma of not making enough money to support myself but making just enough to jeopardize my SSI. When the government sent out stimulus checks at the beginning of the pandemic, the specter of the asset limits once again reared its ugly head. Many people with disabilities who were on SSI feared that the stimulus checks would push them over the asset limit and cause them to lose benefits. The immediate problem was resolved by not counting the stimulus checks as income for a year. But the asset limits had not been adjusted in decades, and there was a bill before Congress to raise them to $10,000. Had this bill passed, it would have offered a more permanent solution.

I joined some colleagues in writing a journal article about the experience of advocating virtually during the DPS, and we wrote the article completely remotely. The pandemic demonstrated just how many things can be done remotely. Since March 2020, I've attended board meetings and gone to conferences. I've collaborated on projects and helped organize events. I've given presentations and participated on panels. I've testified before legislative committees and taken the Oath of Office for a position with a state agency. I've also paid my taxes. And I did all this without ever having to leave my apartment.

The universal embrace of remote work was just one way that accommodations entered the mainstream. In fact, making accommodations was something everyone was forced to do almost overnight. Some events were cancelled, others went online. Businesses changed their hours to abide by limits on public gatherings, and they rearranged their physical spaces to follow social distancing requirements. And everyone had to find alternative ways of spending their time.

There was a seismic shift in how the world operated, and in some cases, even how it looked—such as images of a deserted Times Square. We were all given a new perspective on reality. It was an ideal environment for the development of lateral thinking. Psychologist Edward de Bono coined this term to describe the process of restructuring thought patterns to stimulate creativity. As de Bono explains in *Lateral Thinking: Creativity Step by Step* (1970):

> Lateral thinking is concerned with the generation of new ideas. . . . New ideas are the stuff of change and progress in every field from science to art, from politics to personal happiness. Lateral thinking is also concerned with breaking out of the concept prisons of old ideas. This leads to changes in attitude and approach, to looking in a different way at things which have always been looked at in the same way. Liberation from old ideas and the stimulation of new ideas are twin aspects of lateral thinking. (11–12)

The way that Bedford reworked its annual town meeting was a perfect example of pandemic-inspired lateral thinking. The meeting was traditionally held in the high-school auditorium. Two evenings in March were allotted to tackle what was usually a lengthy agenda. However, because of COVID-19, gathering in an enclosed space for an extended time period was clearly unsafe. Yet, the meeting couldn't just be moved outside or simply cancelled. March can be very cold in Massachusetts, and Bedford had bills to pay that needed to be approved by the town residents. Some rethinking was in order.

Bedford solved the problem by making accommodations. The meeting was postponed until July and held outside on the high-school football field. Chairs were arranged six feet apart to maintain social distancing, and though the meeting began at nine a.m., the agenda was shortened to reduce the amount of time in the hot sun. Only the most essential items were voted on, and the presentations usually given by town committees during the meeting were made available online to be viewed beforehand.

A request for accommodations to improve accessibility is part of Bedford's roots. The town was founded in 1729 by a group of Billerica and Concord residents who lived a great distance from either town's church. When they petitioned the General Court of Massachusetts, they laid out the many hardships they endured because of their remote location and the frequent impassibility of the roads. As Bedford town historian Sharon Lawrence McDonald relates in *A Meetinghouse & Its People: The Story of the First Parish Church in Bedford* (2016):

> Those who lived between the Concord and Shawsheen Rivers were legal residents of Concord or Billerica, and there they paid their taxes, attended church, held offices in town government and participated in civic affairs. The 46 or so families in the area had to travel 5 or 6 miles each way to go to church . . . perhaps in rain, snow, or mud. Church attendance was not optional. Should they remain at home for several Sundays, the tithing man would note their absence and come to collect a fine that could amount to 20 schillings or three hours in the stocks. (2)

I live directly across the street from the marker indicating the old border between Concord and Billerica, which bisects my apartment complex. So, if there were no Bedford, I'd be a resident of Concord or Billerica. And if I wanted to walk to the center of either town, it would take me at least an hour to do so. But there is a Bedford, and I live just off the main thoroughfare called Great Road. And as much as I can accomplish online, I do find it necessary, even beneficial, to venture outside. Blue Ribbon Plaza—where Whole Foods, Bank of America, and Supercuts are located, with CVS directly across the street—is a fifteen-minute walk from my apartment. And the library is only five minutes away.

Still, there are many activities I'm involved in that are not within walking distance, and I appreciate having the ability to attend via Zoom. I think about the meetings I have with colleagues from across the country, sometimes on a bi-weekly basis, and how cumbersome it would be if we only met in person. As the world returns to some semblance of normal, there have been more in-person events, which is cause for celebration. I've already attended several, and I look forward to many more. But as we move forward, I hope that we also keep our virtual options open.

Works Cited

de Bono, Edward. 1970. *Lateral Thinking: Creativity Step by Step*. New York: Harper & Row.

McDonald, Sharon Lawrence. 2016. *A Meetinghouse & Its People: The Story of the First Parish Church in Bedford*. First Parish Church in Bedford.

National Council on Disability. 2022. *Strengthening the HCBS Ecosystem: Responding to Dangers of Congregate Settings during COVID-19*.

7

Ad Astra Per Aspera (To the Stars Through Difficulties)

Brenda Jo Brueggemann

Dear Reader,

Yes, a letter. I am writing you a letter from my deaf-girl-growing-up-in-Kansas heart. I did that quite a lot as a teenager in (extremely rural) western Kansas in the 1970s: I wrote letters. My friends, and my sisters, tended to call each other on the home landline phone and talk for hours every evening after school and dinner—as if they hadn't seen each other for years—from phones that had extension cords a hundred yards long, snaking and tangling through half a dozen different rooms of the house as they chatted on, and on, and on. I wrote letters.

I wrote letters to my friends while pretending to watch TV. (Well, I *watched* TV though I didn't "hear" so much unless I sat down on the thick red shag carpet of our living room and placed myself a foot back from the heavy wood TV console, in strategic lip-reading range and right next to the console's speakers.) I wrote letters sometimes longer than twenty pages of notebook paper in one evening to one particular friend. I feel a little sorry for her now, having to slog through those thick tri-folded letters I left on her desk or in her high-school locker the next morning. But she never complained. She also didn't write back, come to think of it. (The taken-for-granted hearing privilege of lopsided, or non-, communication was real even back then.)

B. J. Brueggemann (✉)
University of Connecticut, Storrs, CT, USA
e-mail: brenda.brueggemann@uconn.edu

I also had "pen pals" I'd never met from several other places around the United States—and even one in Germany for a while that I was so excited about since I had been born in Germany myself, the first child of an Army soldier stationed there. As soon as I received a long-awaited letter from one of them, I would sit down at our kitchen booth, tucking myself in the back corner of it, churn out ten pages back to them, pop it in the mail with embellishments on the back of the envelope, and then wait, always wait, for their slower and shorter replies. Repeat cycle.

When I went to college (for so very many years) I would write home to my grandmother in Tribune, Kansas—who always sent me a short card back with her famous hand-drawn kitties and bunnies in the signature line and a crisp ten-dollar bill, too. Sure, it was the supply line of ten-dollar bills (they went a lot further back in the 1980s than they do now) that kept me writing to her—but it was also that she genuinely expressed excitement and gratitude about receiving my Tales from College missives. In fact, when Grandma Esther died (at the full age of ninety-seven) and we cleaned out her little apartment at an assisted-living complex in Dodge City, Kansas, my son (then a college student himself) was boxing up her books and from almost every book fluttered out a letter—handwritten from me—that she had saved and tucked away. I cried. Actually, my son cried, too. I now have those reclaimed letters—written with pink, green, purple, sky blue, magenta, and sometimes even regular blue or black ink—nestled inside my grandma's own roll-top writing desk that now sits at the front entrance of my home.

My sisters and my mother did not ever—and still don't—write much to me. My text exchanges with them are notably unbalanced, with mine winding on for ten-plus lines, sprinkled with dozens of forms of punctuation, emojis, and emphases. Theirs will come back with one to two lines, an occasional emoji, some comment about the weather (we are always and ever Kansas girls in our running weather commentary). When I spurl a similar tome-ish text to my adult son or daughter these days, there will usually be a pause before my phone lightly vibrates with an incoming text. Their replies—which somehow manage to address all the points in my ten rambling sentences—will be five words. I have no idea how they can do that!

Writing is my passageway. Writing is my pass. Through writing, I pass. I ended one of my first published essays, "On (Almost) Passing," with that claim back in 1997. And it remains, names, and sustains me still.

Also remaining and sustaining for me is the state motto for Kansas, my homeland, my place of origin. *Ad astra per aspera*—"to the stars through difficulties"—is the state slogan for Kansas, domed and arched like the rising sun above the "fruited plain" of farmland on what I believe (with some bias, of course) to be the most stunning state flag in America. (Though Montana runs a close second.) And that Kansas motto feels, to me, to be the most resonant of all fifty options. (Though Idaho's *esto perpetua*—"it is forever"—and Maryland's *fatti maschii, parole femine*—"strong deeds, gentle words"—are slogans I could stand and soar with, too.)

As a "hard-of-hearing" ("deaf" wasn't a word we would dare use back in the 1960s and 1970s) rural western Kansas girl—educated and thriving in a "mainstreamed" environment before there was a thing called "mainstreaming"—and by virtue of the sheer isolation and sparse population of my home place, I soared to the stars, though not without some notable difficulties.

Can I go on, dear reader? You can get a snack, some tea, water, or wine—if you'd like. I'll wait.

I am a first-generation college student (and first-gen faculty member now)—the first (of only a few) of my grandmother's nine grandchildren to go to college. (She used to joke that I got degrees for everyone else in the family—and with five of those and the small mountain of student-loan debt I accrued to go with them, her joke probably wasn't far from the truth.) I grew up in a tiny rural western Kansas farm community on the Kansas-Colorado border; there were only one hundred students in my high school, sixteen in my graduating class, and less than twenty-five people per square mile (with eight times more cattle than humans in the county). My great grandparents were immigrants—Volga Germans, Mennonites—who came to the United States to escape religious persecution and to farm wheat. And there's this, too: for all intents and purposes, medically and socially, I am deaf. "Hard-of-hearing," however, was the hushed-up and doubly-hyphenated term that swirled around me growing up—though never fully to my face.

I entered college, on a writing scholarship (but not for letters!), in 1976 at the University of Kansas—a seven-hour drive away across the flat, largely treeless expanse of the state where the stars truly were stunning and many in the black of our streetlight-free nights. The Milky Way trafficked up there, vibrant and creamy and twinkling, as wide as the four lanes of highway out on Interstate 70 that spanned the state. To the stars . . . but yes, with difficulties. It was only the dawn of Public Law 94-142, The Education for All Handicapped Children Act. Entering college with this new federal legislation at my back, I had no idea, however, what it meant—not at large, not in principle, and definitely not even more specifically for me in my educational and public life. We didn't talk about things like this in western Kansas;

instead, the price of a bushel of wheat, the likelihood of an incoming blizzard, or hailstorm, or tornado, or dust storm—those were the weathered substance of our community conversations. And so, I have often said that I was naturally "mainstreamed" growing up in this remote, protected, and somewhat inaccessible community where just two small and infrequently trafficked two-lane highways intersected at the city limits of Tribune, Kansas 67879, population 900. We played eight-man football in high school and everyone had to participate in almost everything or that thing just didn't exist. No one raised questions then when the deaf girl (who couldn't be called "deaf") played in the school band (a saxophone) or tried out for the junior play (and got a part, too!) or even joined (well, faked her way through) the high-school choir. Always passing, in the mainstream, I played along.

I have also often narrated that I really didn't know I was "deaf" until I went to college at the state's flagship research institution, the (then seemingly, and terrifyingly, immense) University of Kansas. And then, too, I was suddenly, and also terrifyingly, deaf—my difference clanging loudly, like a trail of strung-together empty tin cans, tied to the back belt loop of my jeans. I suddenly talked/sounded different—though many of my seemingly sophisticated eastern Kansas roommates and classmates from the "urban" areas of Topeka, Wichita, Kansas City, even Salina, just thought my lateral lisp and hollow-nasal tone was my western Kansas "accent." Fortunately, they'd never met a deaf person before (nor one from the outposts of way western Kansas either), so they couldn't identify my way of speaking in that frame. I passed, then, even as I clanged with internal anxiety.

Panicked over what I was sure I was missing in my Introduction to Psychology lecture class (with 200 other students in a dark, cavernous auditorium), I arrived half an hour early so that I could always get the front row and center seat right in front of the professor's lectern. (I soon realized, however, that no students ever took those seats anyway—of their own choosing—and so I slept-in the extra thirty minutes.) I brought two other used Intro to Psych textbooks, different from the one my professor required for our class. I read all three textbooks and kept an elaborate cross-referenced and color-coded notebook (three colors, three textbooks) as my substitute for the lecture notes I largely missed. And yes, I aced the class; I was always good at passing in this way, too. As I worked my way through a midwestern university "in the heartland" of America in the late 1970s, I was part of the first generation of "mainstreamed" deaf students, making up our survival and success as we went along. Aiming for the stars, through difficulties.

★ ★ ★

There are so many other stories from this place, dear reader, where my disability—my embodied difference—was first placed, erased, misplaced, spaced. They are like the Milky Way full of stars on a crisp, black winter night out on the Kansas plains. They sparkle and throb together, offering light and awe, but also sometimes overwhelment (a word I made up, yes).

I'll end with just one more from Kansas and one that is also recent. My youngest sister still lives in Kansas—right next door to my mother on a beautiful little spring-fed lake in the Flint Hills, next to the Konza Prairie, the largest remaining prairie land in North America—and other than making her lists of things that need done (groceries to be shopped, birthday cards to buy and send), well, she doesn't write much. Her texts are the shortest of all. She still circulates on Facebook (as many do in rural America), though she is there mostly as a reader and reaction-maker and not much as a post-er herself. Imagine my surprise, then, when I saw her post (with my name tagged so it also appeared on my own Facebook timeline) on the occasion of my sixtieth birthday, which I share with my middle sister who currently lives in Montana. The two of us oldest sisters were born exactly one year apart. (Can't make this stuff up.) Youngest sister, the Kansas sister, wrote the following in honor of our sixtieth and fifty-ninth birthdays:

> *I have two sisters, both born on this very day . . . 1 year apart. They are two of the strongest women in the world today! Yet two of the most delicate. Both in a good way!*
>
> *The oldest has a disability—and because of that, she is the overachiever in the family. Proving herself every chance she gets. She has numerous published books, has been a professor of English and Disability Studies at three esteemed universities, curated a museum display, and is sought by many other universities to "teach their teachers." The list goes on.*

I have to tell you, reader, that my head went swimming with that post and its list, going on. I pushed the "like" reaction thumb at her original page and then promptly deleted the post from appearing on my own timeline. I felt split with difficulties, my head spinning, my heart pounding. I got up and made some calming tea. I looked up the definition of "well-meaning person." I know she meant well—to the stars and all that. And I know that she believed she was honoring me, through my difficulties.

I thought about a term I've invented for my field, Disability Studies: *narrative normalcy*. I often use it when I am teaching disability narratives and memoirs to my students (which is pretty much always). *Narrative normalcy* plots the ways in which we've learned, without much thought to it, to tell a disability story so it eclipses itself with *overcoming* and points always in the direction of *inspiration* (oh, those stars again!). I simply won't let myself believe—through difficulties—that she really thought that everything I'd done in my life was an act of "overachieving" and "because of my disability." She was just adopting a close-at-hand narrative frame that would easily translate to the Facebook Kingdom at large.

She was perhaps herself overcome with "narrative normalcy," not knowing how to tell a story about me, or how to explain my life outside of this long-established framework. Like how to tell a story about Little Red Riding Hood without the Big Bad Wolf? How to narrate about Jack without the beanstalk and the Englishman-eating giant? Or, say, how to spin Cinderella without the evil stepsisters?

She isn't my evil stepsister, though. She is just an extremely good-hearted woman (as I've always called her) trying to finally (sixty years!) openly reference and see the positive and potential (the stars!) in my deafness, the twinkle of my difference—and to proudly acknowledge and even celebrate it on Facebook with all of her friends there (most of whom I don't know, but some of whom are high-school classmates we shared from long ago). She was speaking "out loud"—finally—about a thing that was largely silenced, ignored, set aside as we grew up together on the Kansas high plains, surrounded by wheat and cattle and grain elevators.

Yet in full disclosure: I struggled to accept her bright and twinkling story of my overachieving rise "through difficulties." Let me tell my own story, please.

I posted her Birthday Honor Comment then on the Deaf Academics Facebook group thread. Their reactions were swift and strong, moving in a largely negative space between "sad" and "so very sorry," and "horrified." But positively, too, the conversation that followed also opened up many shared narratives about their own family members' narrative "boxes" for their own deaf lives. We clustered together over these stories, studded with both shine and difficulties.

My native Kansas sister's birthday post, there at the outset of my sixth decade, offered an acknowledgement and a negotiation between what *she* (a bit fixedly) understood or believed about my deafness and its place in my life, set relationally next to how *I* myself place and understand my deaf experience and identity as I slip, I slide, I soar . . . to the stars, with difficulties.

Part II

Metro-Geographies

8

Peaks and Valleys: A Collaborative Essay about Disability in the Bronx

Julia Miele Rodas, Sonia Gonzalez, Annette Serrano,
Cindy Hernandez, Andrew Whyte, Jovan Campbell,
and Mary Morfe

In introducing the accounts that follow—first-person narratives of disability in the Bronx—I am thinking of two things. The first is my commute from Brooklyn, where I live, to my work at Bronx Community College, about fifteen miles to the north. I plan for an hour-and-a-half each way: a quick walk to the R train and down the steps (no elevator at my home station); up steps, through a tunnel, down steps and up steps again at the Atlantic Avenue transit hub, where I change for the uptown number 4 train. This station has elevators, but they're often dirty, frustratingly slow, or simply out of service. Anyway, I'm fortunate not to need them most of the time, and for me, the steps are faster. If I'm lucky, I get a seat on the 4 and mark papers or plan classes during the

---

J. M. Rodas (✉) • A. Serrano • C. Hernandez • A. Whyte
Bronx Community College/City University of New York, Bronx, NY, USA
e-mail: julia.rodas@bcc.cuny.edu

S. Gonzalez
CUNY Graduate Center, New York, NY, USA

J. Campbell
One Heart One Vision, New York, NY, USA

M. Morfe
Bronx Community College/City University of New York, Bronx, NY, USA

CUNY Coalition for Students with Disabilities, Lehman College, Bronx, NY, USA

© The Author(s), under exclusive license to Springer Nature Switzerland AG 2024
S. B. Mintz, G. Fraser (eds.), *Placing Disability*, Literary Disability Studies,
https://doi.org/10.1007/978-3-031-41219-6_8

long ride. I don't usually have any trouble focusing on my work despite the movement and sound of the train, the interruption from announcements, the racket of passengers moving and talking. It's almost like a superpower; I can just tune all of that right out, sometimes only emerging from my work trance as the train emerges onto the beginning of its elevated segment at Yankee Stadium. A few more stops north and I exit at Burnside Avenue, head down a double flight of steps (no elevator at this station), and begin my trek up to the college. The neighborhood is called University Heights with good reason. The half-mile walk from Jerome Avenue where I leave the train to my office on campus includes a 140-foot climb, terminating at one of the highest points in New York City. This steep ascent is typical of the Bronx, where roughly 20,000 years ago, the glacial carving of the Wisconsin Ice Sheet deepened valleys beneath what is now Webster Avenue, giving shape to a dramatically grooved landscape of heights and furrows.

This is the Bronx, the only New York City borough that takes a definite article. "The" Bronx is its own place, much more than a mere geographic zone, defined by geologic features and hedged in by external boundaries. The Bronx is an epicenter of identity, a way of being and a state of mind. Birthplace of hip-hop, home to the Yankees. For many, the Bronx occupies a notorious place in the cultural imagination. Focus often falls on the fires of the 1970s, the crack epidemic in the 1980s, the ongoing realities of poverty and disinvestment. But Bronx pride reaches deep. Bronx celebrity embraces a wide range of accomplishment: Edgar Allan Poe, Calvin Klein, Colin Powell, Sonia Sotomayor. There are expansive parks and gardens, stately architecture, and breathtaking views along the waterfront. The Siwanoy peoples who were the original Bronx inhabitants did not believe in land ownership and fought against the encroachment of Dutch and English settlers in the seventeenth century; later waves of migration shaped neighborhoods, generated microcultures, established schools and places of religion, and gave rise to a rich food culture. Bronx history is Jewish, Italian, Puerto Rican, Black, and in the present moment, decidedly Dominican. The borough is enormously diverse (more than 30% of residents are immigrants to the U.S. and more than half speak a language other than English at home); it's also young (30% of Bronx residents are under 18). Were it independent from New York City, the Bronx would be the ninth most populous city in the U.S.

So, acknowledging the heights and the depths, dynamic culture and history, I return to my second thought, a snippet from *Disability Theory*. Tobin Siebers recalls an outing with friends: "We are in animated conversation," he writes. "We come to the stairs, and my friends, all fitness buffs, instinctively head for them. The elevator is in view. I fight my way up the stairs because I am too embarrassed to ask the others to take the elevator with me and too much in love with good conversation to take it alone" (2008, 51). A momentary pause. My commute and my work for the last fifteen years have made me deeply conscious of the way everyday features of our environment shape disability experience, create opportunities, and present barriers and sites of friction. This passage reminds me, though, that I remain one of the others, not only the commuter from Brooklyn, but also the "fitness buff" who welcomes the steps in the subway, who can tune out the cacophony of the train, and who is energized by the swift, steep hike up to campus. My experience cleaves from that of my co-authors. I journey to the Bronx as I journey to disability, as a visitor, and I come to this collaboration with true respect for the different ways my writing companions approach disability and place.

As evidenced in the following series of brief essays, for disabled Bronx residents, this geography, history, social and cultural context all interact with disability in complex ways. Annette Serrano writes about her experience as a train conductor in the New York City subway system, where a work-related injury left her permanently disabled. As she navigates her new life with a mobility impairment, Serrano shares her fresh perspective on the wild topography of the Bronx, including her take on the iconic "Joker Stairs" located near the 167th Street subway station. In "My Challenges," Cindy Hernandez addresses the exhausting barriers she has faced in her school life, but she also speaks to the ways that Bronx street life impacts her as a disabled person. For Hernandez, one of the most frustrating aspects of her life is having to contend with strangers who feel entitled to interact with her because of her disability. Andrew Whyte is similarly challenged by the constant lively buzz of the Bronx. The thrum of action that so many other residents treasure is a source of intrusion and distraction for Whyte; he ultimately needs to leave his home in the Bronx and relocate to a more tranquil setting in order to maintain his mental health. The inverse experience is related in Sonia Gonzalez's "The Walk-Up." In this essay, the author's brother has moved back to the Bronx; she describes visiting him during the initial, terrifying wave of the COVID-19 pandemic. Like Whyte's writing, Gonzalez's essay is also concerned with psychiatric disability and with the ways the busy, densely packed Bronx can exacerbate the vulnerabilities of people who grapple with psychosis. In the next essay, "A Big Night Out," we return to the theme of the Bronx's monumental hills, as Jovan Campbell shares the difficulties of navigating public transit in a wheelchair.

Campbell's story offers a brutally honest take on what was ultimately a lovely outing, while raising the question of why anyone should have to work so ridiculously hard just to have a little fun. Our collaborative chapter closes with Mary Morfe's "Lemonade in the Bronx." Departing from the focus on barriers and challenges, Morfe's indefatigable sense of joy and gratitude rewrite the Bronx as a hub of disability resources, culture, and ingenuity.

—Julia Miele Rodas

These Steps Are No Joke, by Annette Serrano

Working as a train conductor for the New York City Transit System, I used to move millions of people all over New York City, but I honestly never thought much about the accessibility of the system. Until one day as I was operating my train and the latch that held up the seat in my cab broke off. The heavy, steel seat came crashing down on both my knees. I was in a lot of pain and needed immediate knee surgery, but the city delayed approval for about a year, during which time complications arose because of the way I was walking, causing nerve damage and a bulging disk in my spine. Now, in addition to an operation on my knees, I needed spine surgery. It took four years until I had all the surgeries I needed, and it was a long road to recovery.

During this time, I had to use a wheelchair to move around, leaving me feeling stuck and isolated. When COVID-19 hit and I heard people complaining about not being able to go out and live a "normal" life, I realized that I had already been living that life of isolation for a while. I would not go out unless I had to. I usually went out only when I had a doctor's appointment or had to do grocery shopping, and whenever possible, I did that online and had it shipped to my home, just to limit the time I had to go out. I really had no social life. Navigating the streets of New York City is no easy task, especially in the Bronx. It gave me anxiety to even think about going out. I did not dare go out alone because I was afraid of the hills in the Bronx. I was so scared to fall. How could I go anywhere? I had to walk step-by-step, very slowly; I struggle getting around because my knees and spine will never be the same, and it is hard to bend my knees without pain. Being a person with a disability is a struggle every day. You cannot walk up that hill on Fordham Road without a struggle, and just the thought of walking back down that steep hill is dreadful. I know if I fall and hurt myself, I will not be able to get up without assistance and even more pain. So I avoid that hill all the time. I just do not want to put myself in a situation where I can get hurt.

Even when I realized I was becoming more isolated, even when I had somewhere I really wanted to go, how would I get there when so many stations in the transit system are not accessible? The subway closest to me did not have an elevator, and even when I was able to walk again it was not easy for me to go up or down the stairs. To make things worse, when the train station was crowded, I'd wind up with an impatient line of people behind me, giving me anxiety and making me panic. I remember one day in particular. I had a doctor's appointment downtown. When I finally reached Wall Street, I realized there were no elevators at that station, and as I reached the stairs to leave the station, I saw that it was pouring rain. Since I need one hand to hold the banister and the other to hold my cane for balance, I couldn't open my umbrella. There I was with the rain pouring down on me as I walked slowly, step-by-step, up the stairs. It was so frustrating, and I was close to tears. But when I was halfway up the stairs, a young lady stopped and held her umbrella over me—a gesture of kindness that almost overwhelmed me, I was so grateful.

I used to live on Davidson Avenue, and to get home from the train station there I had to climb these famous stairs, the ones that were featured in the movie *Joker*—nine long stone flights broken up by short landings in between. (Personally, I call these the Stairs of Hell.) The thought of having to face the Joker stairs and then the subway stairs after that! I cannot imagine, even now that I am able to walk again, having to get up those stairs or go down, just to be able to reach the subway. For a wheelchair user, it would have been an impossible task.

It took hard work, determination, and a lot of physical therapy to finally be able to walk with a walker and now with a cane. It has not been easy for me to travel in this city. In my new normal, I navigate the city as best I can, and I'm enjoying this growing sense of freedom and independence, but now that I'm disabled, I realize that public transportation really doesn't serve me well. If you do not have a car, or access to a car, it is really difficult to get around. I stopped taking the trains. I just could not do it anymore. I started taking the bus to get around, and even though I still struggle getting on and off the bus, it is the better choice for me. Recently, I started attending Bronx Community College, and I take the bus every day to get to the campus. Next semester, though, I will be registering for online classes. I'm afraid of the winter months, walking in the snow, risking the slippery sidewalks. I have to think ahead, especially having to deal with going up and down hills.

What used to not be even a thought in my head—accessibility—has become one of the things that I always have to be mindful of: the inaccessibility of the transit system, the hills of the Bronx, even the Joker stairs are really not a joke.

My Challenges, by Cindy Hernandez

Well, hello reader, my name is Cindy, and I'm a student at Bronx Community College. Growing up in the Bronx, I learned many things that help me live a better life with a disability. The most important lesson for me has been that not everybody will understand my situation.

Attending middle school in the Bronx had its challenges. The school building was difficult to navigate due to my limited mobility caused by muscular dystrophy, a condition that causes muscle weakness. The school is on a narrow, one-way street with lots of potholes. And while potholes are part of the Bronx landscape and may not seem worth mentioning for most people, when the sidewalks fill up and street corners swell with students and parents waiting to cross, those potholes can be difficult to see and even more difficult to navigate, especially with weakened muscles that sometimes cause me to be unsteady or lose my balance altogether and fall.

Inside the building, I had to move slowly through the halls and had difficulty climbing stairs. The four-story school does have one elevator, which I know many schools in the Bronx do not have. However, it was often out of service, which meant I had to take the stairs. I remember all those stairs! Even when you first enter the building, there are stairs you must climb just to get to the main lobby where the elevator is located. When the elevator was in service, its use was not monitored, so nondisabled students often used it, making it nearly impossible for me and other disabled students to access it. Because of this, I was often late to class. I remember asking my teachers for permission to leave class a few minutes early so I could get ahead of the crowd and have a little more time to get to my next class, but they usually refused. It was frustrating that they were often impatient with me and unwilling to make accommodations.

Sometimes students were rude and disrespectful to me. Bullies would throw me stuff, call me names, and even push me down the stairs if I couldn't keep up. Teachers would sometimes intervene, but it didn't deter other students very much. And because I couldn't participate in gym, I would sit in a corner watching the kids play, missing out on the joy I saw in them as they ran around and played games.

Navigating the subway and busy streets in my neighborhood is another challenge. Walking up the stairs from the Third Avenue–138th Street station of the 6 train can be stressful, because people often have to wait for me as I slowly climb the stairs. I usually check train times to plan my trip and decide whether to wait for another train if the crowds seem too hard to manage. The intersection where I catch my train is a large, very busy thoroughfare. There are stores and restaurants, churches and apartment buildings, parks and schools—which means lots of people and lots of traffic. As I emerge from the subway, people often push me out of their way as they rush to catch a bus or taxi or make their way to their next destination.

I sometimes feel invisible as people push past me, but there are other times when I feel "overexposed" by a general lack of respect for my privacy. The walk home is typically pretty slow for me because of my mobility impairment, but it's made even slower because people are always trying to stop me to ask questions or pray for my health. If a person has known me and my family for a long time, they stop and ask personal questions. When I feel they are being invasive, though, I simply ignore their questions and continue on my way. Even if they see it as rude, establishing these kinds of boundaries is a priority for my well-being. Not everyone will understand what it's like to live with a disability.

Lost in the Shuffle, by Andrew Whyte

Just about a year ago, I moved to Valhalla, New York, about fifteen miles north of the Bronx. Until then, I had lived in the Bronx for the entire twenty-two years of my life. The difference is vast in where I reside now because I'm able to move at a calmer and more easygoing pace in this environment.

When I lived in the Bronx, everything moved so fast that I felt lost in the shuffle. The overall pace of the Bronx is its own beast. You always see people taking on multiple different things at once. It makes you feel like if you're not also moving at that rate then you're inadequate, not doing or accomplishing anything in your personal life. It makes you rush and have these fast-warped expectations. This unspoken pressure, the expectation of speed and busyness, is a big part of the reason for my psychiatric crises.

I've been hospitalized twice now for schizoaffective disorder. The first time was in 2018, during my first semester at Bronx Community College. I was working for the first time at an afterschool program and going to school at the same time. At first, I was happy, but it was so hard to keep up. I was neglecting my mental health and self-care, and the latenesses and absences started piling up. I just didn't have the time to structure my day and feel balanced and not overwhelmed; and when there was time, I was so fatigued—it's not easy to adjust and adapt at a rapid rate. Soon, I was overwhelmed with depression and anxiety. My second psychiatric crisis happened in 2019, just as I was about to begin my second year working at the same afterschool program for elementary-school children. Again, the stress of having to juggle multiple responsibilities felt overwhelming.

These mental breakdowns put me at a low point. I lost confidence in my intelligence and my abilities, but good therapy through a program called ONTrackNY—and the caring attitude of my family, especially my father—have made me realize that a peaceful, quiet, ordered environment is essential to my mental health. And the Bronx just wasn't a healthy place for me. Even the language of the Bronx moves at its own rapid pace. Most definitely, my home borough has its own creative and expansive and idiosyncratic vernacular: Dub or that's a dub, Bet, Heard, Brick, Bag, Wylin/Wildin', Front/Fronting, Bev, Nah yeah, Yeah nah, Drid, Facts, Good looks, Grimy, and so on. Not much of this language came naturally to me, and the sound of it echoing all around made me feel kind of lost.

In the Bronx, you also have to be alert when you're walking outside. It's not a place where you can walk freely without care. At all times, you have to walk with confidence, with your head held high so you don't become a victim. You have to be cautious, but also not fearful, because if the wrong person comes across you and detects that fear . . . it's easy pickings for them. When I was living in the Bronx, I always had to portray myself as someone I wasn't, pretending I had supreme irrational confidence even in situations where I wasn't feeling confident at all. If I didn't, people might attack me, or, almost as bad, they just wouldn't want to be around me. This constant masking, always putting on a façade . . . it takes a toll.

The stress of putting on a front like this reaches back through high school and even into middle school. Most of my friends had all kinds of *stuff*—the latest phone, the latest sneakers, the latest music, social media, fashion. School was ruled by the Bronx "Dress Code." I will put it in simple terms: the more popular and expensive your clothes, the more attention and respect you got. That's just how it was. Me, personally? I didn't have any swag, and I wasn't dressed well enough to be noticed. Even though I knew a lot about basketball, I couldn't keep up with all the social demands, so naturally, I felt like an outsider in most situations. Unfortunately, this feeling of being an outsider crept over me even at home.

Now that I've moved, I don't have as much noise and distraction around me, and it's easier to manage my mental health. But even though I've left the Bronx, my family has stuck by me. My dad has been the most understanding. As much as I kept pushing him away, he just wasn't going to leave me. He understood the seriousness of what was happening, partly because he'd lost a nephew to suicide. My father didn't care about the stigma around psychosis that is common for people of his generation. He didn't care that mental illness was frowned upon and wasn't looked at as an illness. All he cared about was supporting my recovery. So, I guess my father is one great thing about the Bronx.

The Walk-Up, by Sonia Gonzalez

The elevator is still broken. Hastily applied caution tape is still strung across the wide-open doors. I look down at the four bags of groceries in my hands that feel considerably heavier than when I pulled them out of the car trunk three blocks away—the closest parking I could find. I put the bags on the floor of the lobby and massage the red marks on my hands left by the plastic loops as I glance at the stairs adjacent to the elevator. I sigh, collect two bags in each hand, and start my ascent to the sixth floor. "The penthouse," I think.

In reality, it's a compact one-bedroom apartment on the top floor of a large tenement building on Belmont Avenue in the Bronx, geographically close to Arthur Avenue, but still light years from the borough's famed Little Italy. That's how it is in the Bronx: neighborhoods change from block to block; entire communities often feel ensconced by invisible but still palpable barriers of race, ethnicity, income, and access.

I make my way up the stairs at a steady pace. The bags weigh me down, and the face mask I'm wearing adds to my discomfort, but I am nondisabled and can thankfully manage the trek without much difficulty. I think about this as I take one step at a time, wondering about the tenants in the building with limited mobility. How will they get up and down? How long has the elevator been out of service? It hadn't worked during my visit two weeks ago. How are tenants on higher floors or those who rely on walkers or wheelchairs managing? How will they walk their dogs or just go out for some fresh air and exercise?

Especially now. It is spring of 2020 and we are in the throes of a global pandemic. Billions of people are worried, confined to their homes, unable to go to work and school. Time outside feels like a luxury, and a broken elevator is just one more barrier.

I reach the sixth floor and quickly put the bags down in front of my brother's apartment door. I massage my hands again and give them a little shake to get the blood flowing to my fingertips before knocking on the door. He answers, not wearing his face mask this time. His eyes are wide and anxious. He looks worse than the last time I saw him. For years, he has managed his bipolar disorder successfully, seeing a therapist and taking prescribed medication. After years of turmoil as a teen and young adult, he had finally found what worked for him. Until the start of the pandemic, he had been working full-time, maintaining his mental and physical health, and was happier and more balanced than I'd ever seen him. Until COVID-19 arrived and disrupted the most basic structure and routine in our everyday lives.

This basic structure and daily routine were essential to my brother's well-being, knowing what to expect day in and day out. His daily commute into lower Manhattan for work was well over an hour each way, but he's one of the few people I know who didn't complain about that. It was a routine that grounded his well-being. "I don't mind," he'd say, noting that getting up and leaving the house every day for a job he loved gave him purpose. This was especially true given his line of work. My brother was a case manager for an NYC-based nonprofit. He helped people struggling with mental illness, HIV, and/or substance abuse navigate healthcare, housing, and government assistance. He helped them find their way, as others had helped him find his.

Now, as a result of the pandemic, my brother's routine was shattered. His job—and his mental-health care—had gone fully remote. Abruptly ended were his daily contact and camaraderie with colleagues and interactions with clients, the people he connected with and truly enjoyed helping. Then his hours were reduced. Shortly after, he was furloughed and then laid off. His therapy sessions also went remote, and he admitted that Zoom wasn't working for him. He eventually stopped his sessions. Losing his job, his routine, his therapy—this fractured the disciplined lifestyle he had carved for himself, leaving him vulnerable.

"Hey, how's it going?" I ask, trying to sound casual. I hold out two bags for him to take and step into the apartment.

"Hi, Sonia. It's okay," he replies, glancing nervously into the hall before closing the door. I notice that the living room is dark, even though it's midday. The large windows facing the street that allow for plenty of sunlight are sealed shut, the blinds drawn tight, and the air conditioner is running.

"Tony, it's gorgeous outside! Let's turn the AC off and open these windows. Let some fresh air in," I say, trying to hide my concern as I move toward the windows and begin to open the blinds.

"No, it's fine," he says, moving swiftly to where I'm standing, peeking out the window, and promptly closing the blinds I've just opened. "I prefer it like this."

"Okay." I lean down to pet his dog, an aging but affectionate bichon. "Hey, Brucie," I say, giving him a scratch behind the ears.

I notice a faint smell of urine under the slightly stronger scent of bleach and spot a bucket and mop off to the side. I glance around. The place is tidy and comfortable, as usual, but there's tension in the air. I decide not to ask about the bleach just yet, grabbing the groceries instead, and making my way to the kitchen.

"How are you holding up?" I ask, busying myself by putting away milk, cereal, bread, and coffee. He thanks me for the groceries, and apologizes.

"I'm really sorry," he says, glancing around again. "It's just that with this furlough and all that . . ."

"Hopefully, things will be back to normal soon, and you'll be back at work in no time," I say, trying to lighten the mood. "At least this gives you more time to walk Bruce and get some fresh air."

"I haven't left the house in two weeks, Sonia."

"What?! Why not? What about Bruce? Don't you have to take him out?"

"I just let him go here, in the corner, and clean up after him," he says, motioning to the bucket.

"Tony, that's not good. He's got to get out. *You've* got to get out."

"I can't. It's not safe."

"What do you mean? It's safe to go out. Just maintain space and wear your mask. Besides, the park is right there." I'm talking about the historic 130-acre Crotona Park, recently restored, one of the many beautiful amenities the Bronx has to offer and a decided asset during the pandemic, when we're all afraid to share indoor space.

"It's not that." Tony pauses and looks around again, and I see him shake his head slightly, like he's trying to clear some thoughts. "I think someone wants to hurt me."

I had experienced my brother's mood swings, insomnia, and erratic behavior on and off for years—all our lives, really. I understood that these experiences were manageable and that he'd *been* managing well, but it seemed that the pandemic disruption was spurring a new level of disturbance.

"What are you talking about?" I ask. "Who's trying to hurt you?"

"I don't know. Well, I do know. They live across the street. But I don't know them and I don't know why they have it out for me. Remember I told you people here don't like me? It's getting worse."

I walk to the window and separate the blinds to look across the street.

"Where?" I ask. I think talking—saying it out loud—helps him. He walks over and opens the blinds just enough so I don't have to hold them open, and points.

"Right there, third floor. See the open window? You can hear them."

I can't hear anything, especially with the windows closed, so I raise the blinds a few inches and open the window. The usual noises of the bustling urban street waft into the apartment. I hear the melody of dozens of incomprehensible conversations from people walking by, music from passing cars, honks of horns behind double-parked cars, the occasional dog bark or ambulance siren. Nothing out of the ordinary. I stare hard at the window across the street and listen intently.

Tony had recently moved back to the Bronx from a quieter residential neighborhood on Staten Island. He had appreciated the distance and quiet

Staten Island offered—especially compared to the frenzied pace of Manhattan, Jersey City, and the Bronx, where we grew up. Tony left the Bronx as a teen after difficult middle-school experiences. For him, getting accepted to a performing-arts high school in Manhattan was a kind of salvation. Even decades later, he'd been hesitant about moving back, but he wanted to be closer to me and to our aunt and uncle, who also live in the Bronx. We had both hoped he'd be able to move closer to me, but he wasn't able to find an apartment that accepted his housing subsidy in my neighborhood, so he moved where his benefits were accepted. (Even though Tony had a full-time job, the profound gap between wages and cost of living in NYC made him eligible for subsidized housing.) The advantage of having family nearby had to be weighed not only against what Tony could afford, but also against his feeling of disconnection from the culture of the neighborhood where he eventually found housing—the blare of hip-hop, reggaeton, and salsa through open apartment windows and passing cars; the sound of raucous laughter; and street slang that was not part of Tony's vocabulary. The busyness of his neighborhood was a challenge—the constant hum of conversations, the dense population, and close proximity to neighbors. All this added to the lingering effects of past discrimination, his sometimes literal fights for acceptance as a gay Latino who didn't "fit in" with the culture on Belmont Avenue. Tony has fully understandable feelings of caution about his surroundings, but it's a tension that makes him dangerously vulnerable to paranoia.

"Tony, I don't hear anything."

"You can't hear that?! Seriously?" His intensity startles me. "It's him. The Wolf. He's always yelling at his wife or girlfriend or whatever, and when he gets really angry, he howls like a wolf. He hates me. He hates that I'm gay, hates that I live here. He curses and yells at me from across the street when I go out. Or if he's upstairs, he'll hang out his window, yelling insults whenever he sees me. Now he's got other people in on it. There are two guys that wait in the lobby for me. They don't say anything; they just stare at me if I walk by, and they snicker and mumble under their breath. He tells his girlfriend he's going to kill me, or better yet, make me kill myself. Plausible deniability, you know. Now he's roping in my neighbors in this building. I hear them plotting—"

Tony stops and looks up at the ceiling, panic and anger in his eyes. "They're stalking me," he whispers as he meets my eyes. "I hear them walking up there. I know they're listening. I can hear them through the walls." I look up also and listen quietly.

"I don't hear anyone. And that's the roof, Tony. No one can go up there. Or maybe it's the super or maintenance workers. Did you know the elevator is broken again?"

"Maybe it's the super," he repeats, with a touch of icy sarcasm. "Or maybe it's them listening. I'm not making this up, Sonia—wait, did you hear that?"

"No, I don't hear anything."

"They're mocking you! They're repeating everything you're saying and laughing! God, how do you not hear that!" His eyes are panicked and he starts pacing.

I stay quiet, not wanting to upset him further. This level of paranoia, along with the delusions he seems to be experiencing, are new to me. I look out the window again, across the street, up and down the block, listening, trying to hear what he hears, see what he sees. I look at the ceiling again and hear the window slam shut. He locks it this time and closes the blinds as tightly as they'll go.

"Tony, I'm sorry I don't hear them. I don't know what's going on, but I know you can't stay here, feeling trapped." He's become increasingly agitated and paranoid as the months of mandatory social distancing drag on.

"Forget it, Sonia. It's fine. I'm fine. Thanks for the groceries."

I can tell he's ready for me to leave, so I get my purse, give him a hug, and tell him I'll call him later.

"Yeah, that sounds good. Thanks, Sonia."

As I make my way down the stairs, I worry about my brother. His internalized trauma seems to be manifesting in his paranoia about people on the block wanting to hurt him, but part of this is just where we are, the ordinary sounds of Bronx community rubbing up against the exigencies of the pandemic. I can bring groceries and some reassurance, but little else. As I walk along Belmont Avenue back to my car, I pay more attention than usual to the people I pass. They all seem innocuous. Just people living their lives. I climb into my car, close my eyes, and take a deep breath to settle my nerves, before reaching for my phone to call our father with the latest update.

A Big Night Out, by Jovan Campbell

It's December 2017, and I am looking forward to an amazing night out. My fiancé, Tafari, who has the biggest heart, has gotten us tickets for the "Hot for the Holidays" concert at the Prudential Center in Newark, New Jersey, and I can hardly wait to check out Cardi B, 21 Savage, and Yo Gotti. I also just found out that Lil' Kim, Remi Ma, and Chris Brown are performing, favorites from my younger clubbing days. Tafari and I are both huge music lovers, and even though we've been together for nine years, this is going to be our first big concert together.

While I'm excited about the performance and the night out with my fiancé, I'm also feeling another kind of nervousness and excitement. This is my first big concert since I became blind back in 2007. When I first lost my sight due to diabetic retinopathy, I went through the usual stages of mourning and anger. I was a student at Kingsborough Community College at the time, and becoming disabled was a serious setback. I faced another significant setback when I needed a partial hip removal due to sepsis, and became a part-time wheelchair user. But with my dad's tough love and my family's support, a kidney transplant, and years of orientation and mobility training from Helen Keller Services, I slowly adjusted to who I am now. I've done internships, gone back to college, and even worked with other blind and visually-impaired women to co-found a nonprofit organization—One Heart, One Vision—serving other blind and low-vision women in underrepresented communities. I live better, eat better, and have a better quality of life than when I first started out as a disabled person. Now I'm going to an amazing concert with the man I love, and I know we're going to have a great time.

Except. Getting to the concert turns out to be a giant hassle. Due to my disabilities, the simple task of traveling is often arduous. Unless someone picks me up or cab fare is affordable, I usually need a strategy for making any kind of trip. Sadly, for this reason, I miss many family gatherings. Sometimes I use Access-A-Ride; it means planning my trips at least 24 hours in advance, but unfortunately, I can't take Access-A-Ride to the concert because the destination isn't in New York City. There is also no way we can pay $160 round-trip for a cab. Back when I was living in Queens, I was close to the accessible station at Parsons and Archer, but only 29% of New York City subway stations are accessible, and in the Bronx, the percentage is even lower. Out of the seventy stations in my new home borough, only fifteen are accessible. So, our only transportation options are an $80 taxi each way—or subway and the NJ PATH train. So, our trip begins.

Tafari pushes me to the Kingsbridge station. No elevator. In addition, we are faced with the reality of the Bronx landscape—hills, hills, and more hills. To accommodate the terrain, a big part of the subway system in the Bronx is elevated, and Kingsbridge is an above-ground station with an exorbitant number of steps. It's winter and the night is extremely cold. In general, I hate dealing with winter weather in my wheelchair or with my cane. Snow and ice just create more obstacles. Tonight, the cold makes everything a little more uncomfortable and a little more dangerous. Tafari and I are both concerned I might lose my balance and slip down the stairs, but I make it. The cold also makes Tafari's task—carrying my wheelchair up all those steps—a bit more challenging. From the platform, Tafari tilts my chair back to make sure my front wheels don't get stuck in between the train and the platform. It's stressful and dangerous and time-consuming, but we're both determined to have our special night out.

This is a snapshot of our life together in the Bronx, mostly very happy. We have a great time at the concert despite the hardships we go through to get there.

But I'm not really satisfied just because, for one night, we overcome a bunch of obstacles and have a good time. Most of the time, enduring these hardships isn't beneficial to either of us, and the inability to attend social and family events on a regular basis decreases my quality of life.

Lemonade in the Bronx, by Mary Morfe

In 1998, I moved to the Bronx from the Dominican Republic, and I have lived in the borough ever since. I worked in a factory from 2002 to 2008 as a maintenance worker. It was a physically demanding job that caused long-term damage, including nerve damage in my arm, pinched nerves in my neck, and a hernia in my back. At one point, I was unable to move my right arm for two months. I received medical treatment and attended physical therapy, but due to my injuries, which are lifelong impairments, I was unable to work at the factory. Faced with a lack of steady income to cover rent and other living expenses, I had to apply for public assistance and enter the shelter system in the Bronx. It was a difficult time in my life; however, I found I was able to get the assistance I needed while learning to live with my disability.

For non-locals, the Bronx is probably best known as the home of the New York Yankees. Other noteworthy destinations include the historic Bronx Zoo and the sprawling New York Botanical Garden. Nestled along the Hudson River is Wave Hill, a beautiful public garden, whose pristine landscaping, wooden walkways, and cultural center make you feel miles from the big city. Yet, despite these local treasures, the Bronx remains the poorest county in New York State, with the highest percentage of people living below the poverty level.

People might think this is a problem, but poverty also means that we have a lot of resources here. When I sought help, I was first placed in a general shelter, then transferred to a medical shelter. Through these placements, I was guided through my medical appointments, therapies, and all the paperwork to receive public assistance and food stamps. My social worker even guided me through the application for American citizenship and helped me locate food pantries providing Grab-and-Go, an initiative that helps the Bronx community tackle food insecurity. It turns out that the Bronx is a haven for people requiring public assistance.

After two years, I was referred to a program for people with major depression called the "University Consultation & Treatment Center," which supports people with disabilities integrating back into independent living. When I began this program, I shared an apartment with two other people, all supervised by a social worker. Upon completing the requirements, I was eligible to get my own apartment. I am proud of my experiences in the Bronx, notably how this program guided me in all my goals and helped get me back to independent living.

In 2016, to continue improving my English, I started CLIP, the CUNY Language Immersion Program, and in 2017, I was able to enroll in Bronx Community College and pursue a degree in nutrition. I continued to struggle with disability, but I managed to do well in my first semester. One particular challenge was keeping up with notetaking in class. Because of the nerve damage in my right arm, if I write for too long, my hand begins to hurt and my fingers become numb. In class one day, I noticed a classmate using a smart pen. When I asked about it, she let me know that Disability Services would provide accommodations for students with disabilities. That same day, I visited the office and was grateful to receive accommodations for my disability. Along with other helpful features, the smart pen helped me record my classes, record all the graphs and notes that I wrote on with my smart pen, and translate words into Spanish. Disability Services also helped me with an application for benefits from the Adult Career & Continuing Ed Services-Vocational Rehabilitation (ACCES-VR), which has an office in the Bronx.

I don't want to downplay my own hard work and determination. I've stayed motivated and I've accomplished a lot. First, in 2019, I earned my associate degree from Bronx Community College, graduating with a 3.6 GPA. Then, with the continued help of CUNY, an institution that inspired me to pursue my dreams, I was able to transfer to Lehman College in the Bronx to continue my professional education and earn my bachelor's degree. I graduated from Lehman with honors in 2022 and obtained a B.A. in Dietetics, Foods, and Nutrition, with a minor in Public Health.

None of this has been easy. Disability can be a real challenge, but the important thing is that I didn't do it alone. It's taken a village to help me achieve my goals. In this case, actually, it's taken a borough, my beloved Bronx. With the combined support I've gotten from Disability Services at Bronx Community College and at Lehman, ACCES-VR, and through various Bronx public assistance and mental-health programs, I'm grateful that I've been able to take lemons and make lemonade.

Work Cited

Siebers, Tobin. 2008. *Disability Theory*. Ann Arbor: University of Michigan Press.

9

Blindness and Dyslexia in the Movements of Everyday Life in Toronto

Rod Michalko and Tanya Titchkosky

"I always forget you have a memory," Tanya says to Rod, whose hand gently grasps her elbow as they move out the door of their Toronto apartment. Like all words, these are spoken from and into a context, from and into what Michel Foucault once referred to as the "movements of life" (1973, 25). Not only does life move through a plethora of contexts, locations, geographies, and situations, it also moves with complex and interrelated social positions. Experiencing someone as having a memory and expressing that experience is one such life movement and social position, one that Tanya experiences as part of her dyslexia. Her double-take on memory while moving with Rod, who is blind, through a built environment that does nothing to expect such movement leads to momentary pauses—like hiccups in the flow of what is going on.

These hiccups require a perception-negotiation aimed at securing trust in what we perceive together as the movements of life. The following essay presents various scenes of "moving together," where Tanya's dyslexia and Rod's blindness give rise to perception-negotiations within the urban geographies of Toronto. Mapping the complexities of this movement while walking, shopping, and returning home, we demonstrate the perceptive power of dyslexia

---

R. Michalko (✉) • T. Titchkosky
University of Toronto, Toronto, ON, Canada
e-mail: rod.michalko@utoronto.ca; tanya.titchkosky@utoronto.ca

and blindness as they appear in unexpected ways in everyday life, and also reveal the necessity of orienting to different perceptions as part of the weave of a shared reality.

1.
"I think we turn left at Harbord Street," says Tanya. "Pretty sure it's left."

"It's right," Rod says. "At Harbord, we turn right. The café is a block and half down on this side of the street."

We continue south on Robert Street toward Harbord, Rod's left hand lightly grasping Tanya's right elbow, his right hand inscribing a slight left-to-right, right-to-left arc on the ground in front of him with his white cane. Together we move—one dyslexic, one blind—through the Toronto neighborhood known as The Annex.

"You're sure it's right?" Tanya asks.

"We've been there a thousand times."

"But I don't know how you know we turn right . . . just like that." Tanya snaps her fingers. "I'm always amazed how you do that."

"I'm always amazed that you're amazed. Even if someone told me where something was in Toronto, somewhere I've never been, I'd know where it is."

"You just remember that stuff, don't you?" Tanya says with a little sadness in her voice.

"Yes," says Rod.

"I always forget you have a memory."

Tanya, of course, knows that Rod has a memory, and she is fully aware that memory is an integral part of being human. What, then, is she forgetting? Put another way: what does Tanya's double-consciousness about memory—both forgetting and knowing that it exists in Rod—reveal about specific disabilities in specific locales such as a major Canadian metropolis? In addition, what lessons might emerge about memory, perception, and mobility in the context of navigating the streets of Toronto as a blind and dyslexic couple?

We share with others various ways of perceiving and moving in the world. Without such common-sense understandings, an intersubjective life-world would be impossible (cf. Husserl, 1970; Schutz, 1967; Weiss, 2008). This "life-world" allows for the perception and recognition of different geographies, and different configurations of those geographies (Merleau-Ponty, 1945; McKittrick, 2013). Largely responsible for the sensibility and recognition of different geographies is the assumption of commonly held perception. And, of course, this presupposes a common sensorium, one with all of its parts (senses) working in a way that produces a shared reality—that is, a sensorium that is regarded as ordinary and that functions for all practical purposes (Garfinkel, 1967; Gilroy, 2005). While everyone "sees" the same world, individuals might interpret it in different ways. This is an everyday assumption. And yet, the idea of difference lies buried somewhere deeper. And it is this sense of deeper difference that Tanya's "forgetting" points to.

The trip to the café occasions a discussion of Rod's mental maps based on memories of places he has never seen, in contrast to Tanya's actually seeing these places but without certainty as to where they are. Eventually, we come to Harbord Street. As we do so, two different ways of conceiving movement intersect, and the blind sensorium in its exactitude intersects the sighted sensorium's engagement with the visual feast of a cityscape—with a dyslexic inflection that causes uncertainty about which way to turn. And, then, the large swoop and gentle turn that Tanya and Rod encounter when Robert Street meets Harbord allows neither Tanya to spot the direction to the café nor Rod to feel the turn.

This movement returns us to the lesson that memory must be, at least partially, a sensual enactment of our interrelatedness as we move through social space. Different interpretations of a commonly perceived world do generate different understandings and experiences of that world, some of which conflict (Ricoeur, 1974). But, what of a sensorium that has not received the education of which Paul Gilroy (2005, 42) speaks, or of the sensorium whose education has been disrupted and disturbed by the introduction of a sensorial change such as dyslexia or blindness? What world comes through such a sensorium?

2.
We sit drinking white wine at a favorite Harbord Street café.
"That thing you said earlier was really funny," Rod says.
"What thing?" Tanya asks.
"About forgetting I have a memory."
"Oh, I didn't mean it quite that way."
"I know," Rod says.
Tanya knows that Rod's memory is integral to how he not only navigates the world, but also how he perceives and experiences it. By contrast, memory for Tanya is not nearly as integral. Rod's memory is one of the components of his sensorium, perhaps the main one; this is not the case for Tanya. She does not experience memory as a part of her perceptual apparatus. That Rod uses memory to perceive the world, thus making memory an integral part of his sensorium, is what Tanya "always forgets." Memory is, of course, one of the

ways that people socially achieve and understand a sensible, reasonable world. We are tacitly aware of this world, this taken-for-granted objective reality "just there" for everyone to "see." How we become aware of this world is something that escapes us entirely, though, unless an integral feature of this awareness is disturbed. Disability provides an occasion—a complex opportunity, in fact— to perceive that the world is put together in particular configurations and structures, and that we have implicit methods for understanding the world as "naturally there" (Ahmed, 2006, 35–36). Memory is one such method—one that Tanya always forgets, due largely to her dyslexia and sight, and one that Rod, due largely to his blindness, always remembers and explicitly uses.

This always-forgetting and always-remembering does sometimes generate a sense of separate worlds for us as a couple. At times, when we move about in public together, separate worlds emerge in the midst of a singular, taken-for-granted reality. This is not new, of course, nor is it particular to the commingling of dyslexia and blindness. We often experience "conflicts of interpretation," as Paul Ricoeur puts it, resulting from different perspectives. What is new, however, is that this blend of dyslexia and blindness can be read as an occasion to both recognize and emphasize the cogency of perception— and to understand perception as more than what a typical view of the sensorium and its connection to perception would have us believe. Rather than staying on this typical path of understanding and experiencing dyslexia and blindness as merely cognitive and sensorial distortions, we can follow another path—one that may reveal alternative orientations to the conception of perceptual apparatus, and, more importantly, one that may open the possibility of experiencing dyslexia, blindness, and other disabilities not as facets of second-rate lives (some of which are not worth living), but as the creative richness that exemplifies alternative ways of being in and perceiving the world.

Understanding blindness as the opposite, the distortion, of sight, and understanding dyslexia as distorted readings of space, time, and words, generates an essential conflict among blind people, dyslexic people, and the world. This conflict continues as long as the world and the perception of it remains framed within the scientific and positivistic paradigm of what constitutes reality. The conflict between dyslexia and blindness, if considered as a conflict of perception, may reveal the complex nature of how we—as a couple—put together a world that can't be easily recognized as "just-there" to be perceived.

3.

It's nearly midnight, and we've just attended Thursday bluegrass night at the Tranzac Club. We're making our way down the dimly lighted lane that leads from the 24-hour Metro grocery store to the parking lot at the rear of our apartment building. Rod has two bags of groceries in his right hand, Tanya has the same in her left, and we adjust the way we usually walk together. Rod holds his cane in his left hand rather than in his right, and Tanya grasps his left elbow rather than Rod gripping her right. We adjust our pace and rhythm, as we always do after shopping, and walk slowly home down the uneven, crumbling sidewalk.

Maneuvering out of the store after paying the cashier had taken some doing. Tanya had to make sure there was room for us to pass by grocery shelves, shopping carts, and other shoppers—and then (as if that weren't tricky enough) to negotiate the metal barriers that prevent customers from taking shopping carts out of the store. These barriers allow only one person to pass through at a time. Sideways.

We're "extra wide," as Tanya puts it, with grocery bags on either side of us. Getting through the gates requires careful judgment on Tanya's part. The space is narrow, and misjudgment could lead to an accident. We could bump the gates with our bags and spill our groceries. Worse yet, Rod could smash a knee, hip, or hand. All these risks flash across Tanya's perception as we approach the gates, extra-wide. She feels anxious, no matter how many times we do it.

Rod knows we're approaching the gates, but Tanya still tells him. For most people, passing through is a cinch. Rod knows that no one even thinks about it. No one notices other people doing it. Few have to carefully judge the space between the gates. Fewer still feel any anxiety. We feel these things, Rod knows, things that others don't feel, can't feel, can't even imagine.

Rod can feel his way through. As soon as Tanya lets him know that the gates are within his reach, the dance begins. He lets go of her elbow. Turns his body slightly to the right. Extends the left hand until he touches the left post of the gate. Turns slightly more to the right. Moves the right hand, the one with the bags of groceries, almost directly behind him and, touching the left post of the gate with his left hip, slips through. It's beautiful. Easy. As though we weren't extra-wide—one dyslexic, one blind. Yet we are.

Our perceptions come together in this artful passage. Tanya follows the gates with her sight, Rod with his memory and touch. The two perceptions take in the same things, different things, in different ways at the same time. We pass smoothly through the gates, our movement an imperceptible dance between conflicting perceptions with potential danger. And moving through the gates, along with us, is a sensation of relief and satisfaction. Such movements are our way of life, our *modi vivendi*.

4.

With regard to memory, perception, and imagination in relation to space, Juhani Pallasmaa writes that "We have an innate capacity for remembering and imagining places. Perception, memory and imagination are in constant intersection; the domain of presence fuses into images of memory and fantasy. We keep constructing an immense city of evocation and remembrance, and all the cities we have visited are precincts in the metropolis of the mind" (2005, 67). The sameness and difference between Tanya and Rod's perception of moving through Toronto (or anywhere) together is steeped in just these intersections of perception, memory, and imagination. It isn't that Rod uses memory to perceive and move in an environment while Tanya does not; nor is it just that Tanya uses sight while Rod does not. Whether innate or not, we all have the capacity to remember spaces, as Pallasmaa suggests. We move in "the domain of presence" that space "fuses" in memory and fantasy to create an image of the space. So as we travel between the Metro grocery store and our apartment building, the "reality" of that space as we experience it blends our memories and fantasies, choreographing the dance that symbolizes our movement together (Esteban, 2022).

Tanya's perception intersects with her memory as it does for everyone, whether we think we have a good memory or not. How Tanya imagines a space intersects with where she remembers that space to be, and what she remembers it to be for herself and Rod, as well as for others. All of these intersecting points (perception, memory, and imagination) are bathed in sight, thus rendering Tanya's intersection-of-perception an aspect of "the visual." But it is the visual "seen" by Tanya through the relation of moving with Rod's blindness, a visualized blindness, one that can be both distant from and intimate with Rod's experience of blindness.

Rod's perception, too, intersects with his memory. Unlike Tanya's perception-memory intersection, his is not tacit. It is an explicit evocation. Rod evokes his memory of the walk between the store and the apartment building, and he evokes, too, his memory of similar walks in similar spaces. Unlike Tanya, though, his intersection-of-perception is not bathed in sight. His memory is imagined in relation to Tanya's memory—a memory perhaps slipping away, perhaps a memory distracted. Or perhaps she will stay the course of their routine movement.

Sight is present in Rod's intersection, in much the same way that memory is present in Tanya's. Together, our perceptions intersect, and as we move together in Toronto, we construct "an immense city of evocation and remembrance." Our "immense city" has its "precincts" together with memories and images of other cities. The "metropolis" that we have constructed resides in the "mind" insofar as it begins in imagination. We imagine not only abstract movement, but also movement oriented to the imagination of moving blind and dyslexic. We both imagine these movements. The precincts in our metropolis are formed by imagination experienced as the structural movements of dyslexia and blindness, and of the commingling of these movements as they wend their way through the city. The immensity of the city materializes at the turn onto Harbord Street; in the memory of left and the uncertainty of right; in the movement through the Metro gate; in the walk down the lane to our apartment building. *This* immensity might only be available to those who move in a metropolis built from a dyslexic and blind sensorium as it builds an imagined presence that fuses movement with precincts. Still, in this movement we become part of the environment.

And, on we move.

5.

The laneway is dark and eerily silent, even though it's a mere half-block off busy Bloor Street. Tanya always notices these features, especially late at night. She notices them now as she and Rod move down the laneway toward home, groceries in hand. Tanya is also aware of the terrain. She focuses on the dips in the surface of the pavement and the broken pieces of cement scattered here and there.

"Bumpy underfoot," she says, "little curb," reminding Rod of surface irregularities he might trip on.

It's funny, Rod thinks, how darkness quiets a city (not quite as dramatic as the quiet of fresh fallen snow). He listens to this silence as they make their way home down the laneway, focusing on the surface of the pavement, feeling for irregularities with his sneaker-clad feet. His memory joins his hearing and touch to perceive the pathway home. With Tanya's touch on his left arm and her descriptions, he feels confident and secure.

That's weird, Rod thinks. *A delivery truck? . . . Maybe, but a delivery truck would be closer to Metro. A car? With a messed-up muffler?* Whatever it is, it's coming up behind.

Plenty of room, Tanya thinks. *Lots of room for that car to pass. Funny how it snuck up. It hardly made a sound. Lots of room to go by us, though. Still, be sure—check over your shoulder.*

Suddenly, Tanya's hand is gone. Rod no longer feels it on his arm. Thump! Then the sound of grocery bags hitting the pavement . . .

"Tanya! Where are you? Are you alright? Tanya!"

Rod moves to his left, stoops and feels with his cane and feet. He keeps asking where she is and whether she's alright. He thinks he heard her say something just as the vehicle swept by on his right.

"I'm fine; I'm fine. Give me a second," Tanya says, finally.

"What happened?"

"I'm okay. I just tripped on something. Don't be angry."

"I thought you were hit by a car!"

She groans a little and starts to laugh. Then Rod starts to laugh. And then they start to search for their groceries, scattered at their feet.

There is, in this laughter, the startling experience of two different senses of what happened being stitched back into one shared reality. But before the laughter, there was confusion: Tanya wondered about the angry question from Rod, and thought, *Where's the sympathy for taking a spill?* Rod, meanwhile, wondered why Tanya hadn't told him what happened—if she'd been hit by the car and badly hurt. Into this social geography, a split, a gap, a wrinkle of uncertainty was inserted—which laughter served both to highlight and to make less powerful (Al-Saji, 2018).

When Tanya tripped and fell, they both experienced a tear in their image of moving together. The laughter helped Tanya understand that Rod wasn't angry but afraid; he thought she'd been hurt by the vehicle he heard—a vehicle Tanya forgot she too had heard when she tripped and fell, spilling the groceries. The sound of the vehicle was no longer available to Tanya as a way to make sense of the emotional intensity of Rod's questions. The loss of contact between them thus meant, if only momentarily, two very different things: a fall marked by a lack of sympathy, and an accident striking in its uncertainty.

Retrieving the groceries, laughing, realizing that we had different senses of what had happened—all this began the process of stitching the imagined fabric of the city back together so that we could resume our journey home. One dyslexic, one blind, moving together in the fabric of our togetherness, stitched less with touch and sight than with an intimacy of space in which dyslexia and blindness make, *are*, home.

Works Cited

Ahmed, Sara. 2006. *Queer Phenomenology: Orientations, Objects, Others*. Durham: Duke University Press.

Al-Saji, A. 2018. "Hesitation as Philosophical Method—Travel Bans, Colonial Durations, and the Affective Weight of the Past." *The Journal of Speculative Philosophy* 32 (3): 331–359.

Esteban, J.M. 2022. "The Inspirations of Our Remembering: My Dance with Katherine Dunahm, Our Dance with the Itch of Disability." *Journal of Literary & Cultural Disability Studies* 16 (1): 93–107.

Foucault, Michel. 1973. *The Birth of the Clinic: An Archaeology of Medical Perception*. Trans. A. Sheridan. London: Routledge.

Garfinkel, Harold. 1967. *Studies in Ethnomethodology*. London: Polity.

Gilory, Paul. 2005. *Postcolonial Melancholia*. New York: Columbia University Press.

Husserl, Edmund. 1970. *The Crisis of European Sciences and Transcendental Phenomenology: An Introduction to Phenomenological Philosophy*. Evanston: Northwestern University Press.

McKittrick, Katherine. 2013. "Plantation Futures." *Small Axe* 17 (3): 1–15.

Merleau-Ponty, Maurice. 1945. *Phenomenology of Perception*. Gallimard edition. London: Routledge & Kegan Paul.

Pallasmaa, Juhani. 2005. *The Eyes of the Skin: Architecture and the Senses*. West Sussex: John Wiley & Sons Ltd.

Ricoeur, Paul. 1974. *The Conflict of Interpretations*. Evanston: Northwestern University Press.

Schutz, Alfred. 1967. *Phenomenology of the Social World*. Evanston: Northwestern University Press.

Weiss, Gail. 2008. *Refiguring the Ordinary*. Bloomington: Indiana University Press.

10

Disability in New York City Schools and Preparing Teachers to Work in Them

Laurie Rabinowitz

In my early years as an elementary-school special educator in East Harlem, I developed an awareness of the issues that systematically disenfranchise students who live at the intersections of multiple marginalized identity categories, including students with disabilities. At that time, I lived in a middle- and upper-income neighborhood, south of my school on Manhattan's Upper East Side, and would often walk to and from work, passing several New York City public schools along the way. As I traveled, I observed the racial segregation of the schools, which came as no surprise given the sociology classes that I had taken as an undergraduate student and my schooling experiences in suburban New Jersey. What I did not know before I started teaching was that students of color are overrepresented in special education (Annamma et al., 2016), and how closely linked that overrepresentation was to the geographic context of a school and the socioeconomic background of the students enrolled in it.

As I researched the schools in the neighborhoods around my apartment, I discovered that the schools to the south of where I lived, which enrolled far more white students than students of color, had fewer students with disability classifications. To the north, however, in the direction of the school where I worked, the trend reversed. In schools that almost exclusively educated students of color, and where the students were increasingly poor, there were significantly more students with disability classifications.

L. Rabinowitz (✉)
Skidmore College, Saratoga Springs, NY, USA
e-mail: lrabinowitz@skidmore.edu

At that time, I thought of disabilities as natural, medical embodiments, so I was perplexed. Where was this trend coming from? Why wasn't this trend a topic of discussion in the courses I had been taking to become a special-education teacher? I had few tools for making sense of the pattern that I was witnessing, and the tools that I did have came directly from the mainstream special-education research base, which uses a medical model for theorizing disability. In other words, I had been taught that students, like patients in a doctor's office, may come to school with educational problems and that it is the job of the school's scientific expert, the psychologist, to assess children to classify their disabilities. Students were then to receive treatment in the form of special education with annual follow-up to assess progress (Valle and Connor, 2019). Given this mindset, I was left to explain the overrepresentation of low-income students of color in special-education settings with theoretical models that assumed a deficit within my students.

But in fact, many of my students were experiencing disabling conditions brought on by accountability culture in the New York City schools. I'll offer just one of many examples to illustrate this point. The staff of the small East Harlem elementary school where I worked was perennially afraid (and rightfully so) of being closed by the city. We feared what closing the school would do to the low-income, predominantly Latinx and Black community that we served. In addition to relying on the school for the education of their children, many of the families in our community also trusted our school as a resource to help meet basic needs. We worried about the impact that closing the school would have on our students—who, in playing on the school's basketball team or imagining what it would be like to walk across the stage during their fifth-grade graduation, had a deep sense of pride in the school they attended. We considered our own jobs and how hard it would be to start again in a new school, and we thought about losing the trust that we had built between each other and the families that we served.

We also knew that the scores our students received on the New York State exams were a significant factor in keeping our school open. The higher the students scored, the more likely that would be. The administrators and faculty made strategic decisions during testing season. Teaching the students who were "on the cusp" was a common strategy. This meant that teachers focused their instructional attention heavily on the students who they believed could jump a level on their state exam scores with six to eight weeks of targeted test-readiness instruction. Often, these were not students with disability classifications. This approach meant that many of the students with disabilities would receive less academic attention during the crunch time before the exams.

Their educators were busy trying to keep the school open by offering test-prep instruction to those on the so-called cusp.

This whole process—the fear of the school closing because of test scores, the attendant focus on educating students on the cusp, and the resulting loss of focused instructional time for students with disabilities—did not happen in the same way at the schools closer to my apartment. Yes, those schools may have been concerned with test scores. Yes, they may have modified their curriculum as the tests approached. But power and privilege often ensured that students with disabilities were still properly educated. In New York City, wealthy families are more likely to successfully advocate for a child with a disability because they can more easily access legal counsel. Because the Individuals with Disabilities Education Improvement Act (IDEIA) of 2004, a federal law, mandates that every child with a disability receives a Free Appropriate Public Education (FAPE), families who have access to this information come forward to demand that this education is provided (IDEA, 2022).

I knew a great deal about this context as a special-education teacher in East Harlem. Yet, despite having these lived experiences of how the social system was directly disabling my students, I still perceived of disability in terms of embodiment. The inability to perceive of disability as a social construct left me utterly confused about how to address the disabling conditions many of my students were experiencing.

In that time, I sought out higher education to better understand the context in which I was teaching and the connections between social class, race, disability, and locale—where, that is, students lived on the grid. After earning two master's degrees in education, however, I was still left grasping for understanding. It wasn't until I started my doctoral program and became exposed to more critical theoretical frameworks—such as Disability Studies in Education (DSE), Inclusive Education, and Disability Studies and Critical Race Theory in Education (DisCrit)—that I understood how disability could be simultaneously embodied and socially produced through a complex embodiment stance (Siebers, 2013). I came to learn that racism and ableism are interconnected and mutually reinforcing, and that I could reimagine my teaching and the teaching of other special educators to consider how racism and ableism coexist in educational institutions.

These ways of thinking offered me a way to understand my past teaching, and they bolstered my work as I transitioned to a Brooklyn-based charter school as a director of instruction. This school exclusively used an integration-based model for special education, within a student body comprised predominantly of students of color. Here, students with disabilities were not segregated into separate environments, but instead spent much of their school day receiving special-education services in general-education classrooms. Yet, in this new setting, with my new theoretical understandings, I still felt frustrated. Why had I never explored the idea that a society's responses to disability determine a disabled person's experiences and outcomes? Why had this way of thinking been absent from my teacher education? To which educators were these frameworks made available, and why? How did educators who learned how to teach using these frameworks sustain their work in schools like mine? By entering the field of teacher education, I joined the ranks of scholars of DSE, Inclusive Ed, and DisCrit, with the goal of shifting how educators understand disability.

When I transitioned from elementary-school-based work to higher education, I became a teacher educator who prepared teachers to be actively anti-ableist and antiracist in their practice. In the same way that the geographies and conditions of specific places had influenced my understanding of my teaching practice, location played a key role in my early years in teacher education. Many of the novice teachers with whom I was working identified, like myself, as able-bodied, and they were not aware of the circulation of "everyday, subtle, intentional—and oftentimes unintentional—interactions or behaviors that communicate . . . bias" towards disabled people (Limbong, 2019). I devised a series of scenarios to help new special-education teachers identify the ableism inherent in some of the everyday language and actions in their environments.

For me, commuting the five boroughs of New York brings about both freedom and hassle. I have always loved the easygoing nature of New York City transit, where one can read a book, listen to music, people-watch, or even take a nap. But this form of travel also makes one dependent on community. Commuters are often stuck waiting for a subway car that feels like it will never arrive, or they get caught in traffic as a bus driver honks through a gridlocked intersection. Knowing this shared background, semester after semester, I asked my students to analyze the microaggression of someone rolling their eyes or sighing when a person with a wheelchair gets on a bus. For many of my students, this example offered a moment of reckoning. They knew that the buses were the city's most accessible form of transportation for wheelchair users, and that they had also been the person sighing over the fear of being late. It takes time, of course, for a bus driver to lower the ramp and then secure a wheelchair using specially designed tether straps. Analyzing this shared experience of negotiating the city buses offered my students a way to recognize their able-bodied privilege.

While I became skilled at using the shared knowledge of transit in my locality to educate my students about ableism, my naiveté (or my New Yorker egocentrism) got the better of me. I interviewed for a job at a school in suburban southern New Jersey—a context that I should have known well from my childhood. When I used the bus-transit example of microaggression during my teaching demonstration, the students stared at me blankly, blinking their eyes. Eventually, one student revealed that she had never ridden a public bus and did not understand the problem.

Such moments of disruption help me learn. At this point, I knew that disability was socially constructed through environment. This demonstration lesson further illuminated for me that the place where disability happens matters deeply. The comingling of wheelchair and non-wheelchair users in the transit system was not something the students in southern New Jersey were familiar with, which also meant that they were unfamiliar with the harm caused when able-bodied passengers roll their eyes at a wheelchair user. I came to understand that I needed to be a better student not only of my own environment but also of the environments and geographies of all the special-education teachers I was going to prepare. I needed to support them in understanding how ableism circulated in their own as well as our shared contexts.

Some years later, I had the dizzying opportunity to supervise a teacher during her master's program in one of the schools that I used to pass on my early-career walks to work. In fact, this school was across the street from my former apartment building. It just so happens, in typical New York City style, that this building actually contains two schools. School and city officials are always seeking out solutions to the limitations of space on the island of Manhattan. (I myself have only worked in cohabited public-school buildings.) So, I happened to visit this building to observe Sophie, a special educator, teach in the school next to my former apartment on the Upper East Side. The school has two entrances—the avenue side and the playground side. The entrance that faces the avenue is a gifted-and-talented labeled school, and its entrance is four beautiful glass doors inviting students, teachers, and visitors into the building. Not surprisingly, the school enrolls very few students with disabilities.

On the back side of the building, facing the playground and not viewable from the avenue, is a second entrance—a set of heavy, metal fire doors painted in faded beige. Inside, one finds a traditional public school where nearly one quarter of the student body has some form of disability. These schools are in the same building, in the exact same spot in the city, but they serve different communities.

To be clear, I do not fault the educators who work at these schools or the families who send their children to them for the social phenomenon I am describing. Visiting Sophie's co-taught general education/special education integrated classroom, I saw two teachers and two paraprofessionals working hard to support all the students with whom they worked. I saw lovely, thoughtful children cultivating their reading, writing, and mathematics skills. I also watched this community Zoom into one another's homes when the COVID-19 pandemic arrived in New York.

It is not the individual actors or their behaviors that have created this segregated schooling experience for students with disabilities. In New York City, we have long sustained a schooling system that places students with disabilities behind windowless, beige doors, while those deemed gifted enter through a polished glass entrance at the front of the building. In contrast to when I first started teaching, I now had a much stronger understanding of what was producing this school segregation. I was able to use my theoretical tools to help Sophie make sense of her experience. Sophie was teaching a tricky student that year, one who had experienced housing insecurity and was demonstrating behaviors that challenged his learning and the learning of his peers. Sophie and I worked together to understand the context that produced the student's behaviors, so that she could seek out resources and provide the support that he needed. Together, we came to recognize that his behavioral struggles were the result of external trauma, rather than an internal problem that needed to be fixed.

Over the years, these experiences have led me to reflect more deeply on my early-career walks to work and how they played an essential role in developing my understanding of disability. As a teacher educator who supports novice teachers, emphasizing place has started to take on new significance. I took my advisees on a community walk last year, and we held our first few classes outside in a local garden. In part, this was to build relationships with one another without wearing masks in the era of the COVID-19 pandemic. But it was also because I wanted to emphasize how working with students with disabilities is a job embedded within locality. We explored the assets around their graduate school. We talked to people on the street. We used location to get to know one another. We discovered that one of the students in our class was a member of a religious institution in the community. We discovered that another member of our group lived just a few blocks from campus. All this information helped us to better situate how we would learn together during the rest of the academic year.

While my advisees responded positively to our project of exploring the community as a learning experience, they found it harder to pinpoint how disability and the education of students with disabilities are tied to location. Several asked me how they could use a community walk to get to know their students when their students were bussed to their school from a different community—which is not uncommon among students with disabilities. We talked about displacement and how systemic responses to disability often move disabled bodies and minds to new, often unfamiliar geographies. We asked ourselves questions: How do we make sense of our students knowing that their disability is a reason for movement across geographies? Is going to school in one's home community a privilege? With inquiries such as these, I now encourage novice teachers to walk the neighborhoods of their schools and their homes, and to ask themselves about the experiences of disabled people in those communities.

Works Cited

Annamma, Subini Ancy, Beth A. Ferri, and David J. Connor. 2016. "Touchstone Text: Dis/Ability Critical Race Studies (DisCrit): Theorizing at the Intersections of Race and Dis/Ability." In *DisCrit: Disability Studies and Critical Race Theory in Education*, ed. Subini Ancy Annamma, Beth A. Ferri, and David J. Connor, 9–32. New York: Teachers College Press.

Individuals with Disabilities Education Act (IDEA). 2022. https://sites.ed.gov/idea/

Limbong, Andrew. 2019. "Microaggressions Are a Big Deal: How to Talk Them Out and When to Walk Away." *National Public Radio WNYC*. https://www.npr.org/2020/06/08/872371063/microaggressions-are-a-big-deal-how-to-talk-them-out-and-when-to-walk-away

Siebers, Tobin. 2013. "Disability and the Theory of Complex Embodiment: For Identity Politics in the New Register." In *The Disability Studies Reader*, ed. Lennard J. Davis, 5th ed., 278–297. New York: Routledge.

Valle, Jan W., and David J. Connor. 2019. *Rethinking Disability: A Disability Studies Approach to Inclusive Practices*. New York: Routledge. 2nd ed.

11

Drenched Lands, Blood Compost: Disability, Land, and The Asylum Project

Petra Kuppers

> the stink of beginnings and endings
> —Larissa Lai, (2002) *Salt Fish Girl*

Blood Meal

Blood meal is dry
inert powder blood
high-nitrogen organic fertilizer
high-protein animal feed
N = 13.25%.
P = 1.0%.
K = 0.6%.
one of the highest non-synthetic
sources of nitrogen
from cattle or hogs
slaughterhouse by-product

P. Kuppers (✉)
University of Michigan, Ann Arbor, MI, USA
e-mail: petra@umich.edu

Fields

I visited Eloise, a closed-down asylum and poorhouse on the outskirts of Detroit. A local historian led my class through hallways in the administrative building, showing glass cases with mementos.

And at the end of the day, we walked out onto the mud field where the dead of Eloise are buried, without gravestones. Thick fields. What did we expect to see?

In defining the performative stance he calls "The Custodian's Rip-Off," Dwight Conquergood (1985) discusses the practice of taking what we find and making it our own, using other cultures, other people, other pain as material for our production. Are we here as part of a rip-off trip? How can we find something of value here, something that speaks about missed dialogues, a respectful meeting with the dead?

We walked about, full of gothic imaginations, of hidden signals, looked for gray concrete markers, and lost our footing. My cane slid off rain-slicked surfaces heaving up from the mud.

I am disabled, and it hurt me to walk. I walked longer than I usually do: maybe I envisioned a form of payment, a penance for disturbing the dead: a bit of bone dust, a crystal's edge in the geode of my riven joint. I am revisiting these words, written years ago in a café after dropping my students off in town, and the words read differently to me now, after the 2020 news of Indigenous children's mass graves found on the grounds of Canadian residential schools. My initial explorations predated my growing awareness of disability's incarcerated entanglement with other colonial and capitalist precarities, but the awareness blossoms into my presence in this writing now. This is one of the gifts of the dead: memory, and its function as connective tissue, malleable, open to new influence. I revisit Eloise, and with it, create new pathways, connect land to land. I write toward stories of demarcation: the mad and ill here, Indigenous peoples here, redlining here: connections between modernist divisions, laid out as landmarks, there for us to find with our stumbling feet.

That day, the graves could not be found. We found the trimmed and proper cemeteries, but what about the unmarked, the 7,000 bodies hidden somewhere in that square mile of land? The ground was so muddy, so moist, I expected things to resurface. When my cane sank inches into the mud, I imagined it hitting something hard, a tombstone, a coffin, a bone. But the sunlight was thick and the wind was relentless and we couldn't find the graves.

Compost

Compact container for contemporary kitchens.
Gray medical-looking device
(think used insulin syringes in casino restrooms)
snaps shut.
Smell of coffee grounds, orange peels, avocado skins.
Spicier, deeper scents beneath.
To take too full a whiff might constrict the throat:
threat.
Abeyance.
Worm homunculi seeding from horseshit's effluvia.
White egg-shell crunch.
Barista memories: labor in the coffee factory
damp discards next to new
disks of tampered brown grounds.
Supply chains connect three coasts
ivory memories, Brazilian forests, highlands.
Precious seeds laid out in the sun to dry.
Short gathering season.
Dark snow, winter mud,
cold brewed grounds siphoned
through recycled brown paper filters.

Children of the Compost

Camille (a fictional entity of the Children of the Compost, a collaborative web of speculative narratives hosted by feminist theorist Donna Haraway [2016]) came into being at a moment of an unexpected but powerful, interlaced, planet-wide eruption of numerous communities of a few hundred people each, who felt moved to migrate to ruined places and work with human and nonhuman partners to heal these places, building networks, pathways, nodes, and webs of and for a newly habitable world (Haraway, 137).

For our *Asylum Project* performance research (2016–20), my fellow disability culture activist Stephanie Heit and I worked with communities in many locations—multiple sites in London, New York, Belgium, Netherlands, Norway, California, and elsewhere. We explored meanings of "asylum"—from nation-state sanction to refugee status, from mental-health institution to religious sanctuary, from lesbian bars to forests. In each of these workshops, small temporary communities formed in acts of creation, poetic exploration, situationist drifting, communal psycho-geographies, urgent languages, and feelings grown anew out of the detritus of history. These communities assembled for short moments of time: a week here, a day-workshop there. In each session, we touched the conditions for making community, in touch with and respectfully on Indigenous lands, aware of our own histories as immigrants and white settlers.

Field Work

fake sunshine: heatlamp wind
incubate, infiltrate
inoculate medical invention
TB patients' bone meal
deep beneath my feet
smell of yellow
stringy weeds
last season's dead seeds
hair across the land

The Dunes

Dunes are unstable land. Protected wildlife, precarious flowers, shrubs, do not walk here, dune grass ready to un-anchor, shift down the steep hill, fill in where your knee has skinned itself on your ascent.

Duin en Bosch, founded 1909: dunes and bush, this is land on the edge of reclamation and naming. The ocean roars just a tad further out, whitecaps mark submerged hillocks, calmer edges, turbulence. The asylum's "design reflected the attempt to control difficult patients and the marginalization of the most difficult patients to the outskirts of the grounds" (Onrust, 1993, 92).

The wind scours all thought out of the twisted trees that find a home here. Long, straight bike-riding trails fit for my wheelchair, slowly undulating into the history of this place. One of the big Netherland psychiatric institutions has found roots here, anchored itself to the edge of the sea. Something about the edge of wild and civil, claimed and open, gives sanctuary or security, depending on which side of the guard house you're on. Are you the policeman with the painted shutters, guarding the entrance against penetration, from within and without? Or are you the inmate, overloaded, willing to retreat into a room of gray, a world of monochrome, wind, and sea mist?

Bubbles by the seaside. I look at the dune hollows. Remember youth dates, backs arcing out circles of kisses in the sand. I was a young German girl whose family drove the few hours to the seaside here each year, and I grew up swimming in these shallow seas. One of my lovers was a young soldier, a poet, whose book I still have: *Dar Var Flinders Starven* (*Where the Butterflies Die*). It's in Flemish Dutch, and I deciphered some of the poems, without flow for me in my other tongues. But those nights, in the dunes, we poured ourselves into the earth and the sand, sea in our back, young liquids mix well with disco highballs.

He was a soldier because that is what one did when I was a teen; young men were drafted into national service. All men were soldiers, all women were not, and that never made sense, for any of us. The gender division was starker here than in any other realm: clothing or demeanor, future dreams or histories of assault.

Before my life with my wife Stephanie, I had not been with someone with long histories of psychiatric institutionalization. I had known nuns, and soldiers in their barracks, all in their own histories of confinement and accepted walls. Lots of us disabled people, including myself, with months of hospital stories. But not the madhouse, the asylum, the inside of the bleak spaces reimagined as safety site, as a hovering place to keep the outside out and open the insides to one's ownership. So I am learning new ways of appreciating the sites of asylums. No longer do I think of Duin en Bosch just as apart, as thrown out, as lost coast.

My love has entered walls like these because she needed to, to retreat and hear the lock turn behind her. So I think Laputa, the floating island, the country that un-anchors from the known and the familiar. Lying in the air, with dunces' caps, its own rules, and patterns of behavior. To look out at the gentle land, dunes rising and falling, shifting, gives a new temporality to the presumed stability of land. Here, much land is reclaimed from the sea: polders drain the fields, desalinate what otherwise might be grazing grounds for sea cows, old mermaids, not the Oreo cows, the black-and-whites. Think fens. Think flood. Think milk and slaughterhouse blood.

All changes, but behind the tight octet of glazed eyes, windows in brick walls, there might be a stable moment. Hum, birdsong, murmur of sea's presence. Breath against the cool damp air. A hint of ion, salt air, expanding the lungs. Boundaries slightly smudged, a gray-blue-green watercolor of a map.

Walt Whitman (from "This Compost!")

Behold this compost! behold it well!
Perhaps every mite has once form'd part of a sick
person—Yet behold!
The grass covers the prairies.

Adinkerke

Adinkerke Military Cemetery is a Commonwealth War Graves Commission (CWGC), a graveyard for the dead of the First and Second World Wars.

Before our Duin en Bosch visit, Stephanie and I slept for a few nights in a tiny cramped caravan near De Panne, Belgium. The area is part of a long strip of coast where I had spent many childhood summers, twenty kilometers from Dunkirk, a town in which over 1,000 civilians were killed by German bombs in the battles.

On one of my adult trips back to De Panne, one member of our travel party was an older man, British, not a family member, a veteran of WWII. We all went together to Adinkerke, to pay respects.

The dune landscapes hide flashes of battles, of dying men, of soaked blood, of rape in villages. There are too many elegies of the mixing of fluids, ocean, and blood, with the sandy soil of battlegrounds. It was easy to find ordinance in the sands when I was a child. Accidentally exposed unexploded bombs were written about in the local papers each summer. Dune memories. And I remember my grandfather, who lived in our three-generation home with my parents, his wife, and my sister and me. He had only one leg: one had been amputated after his incarceration as a prisoner of war by Russian forces, after the end of WWII. He knew where his leg was buried.

Most of the disabled people I knew as I grew up were Kriegsversehrte: the war wounded. They had a narrative stitched into their wounds, their missing limbs. It is a harsh narrative, as they had been Hitler's soldiers, whether as conscripts or volunteers. Shame hung in the living rooms, and in the pubs. My grandfather certainly never told us grandchildren of his experiences on the Russian front, of his years as a prisoner, of how he came to come home—or of his cousin, also a war prisoner, who didn't.

This is a different disability shame from the one I learned so much about when I began to learn about disability studies from the British teachers of the

Open University. But it was there, and I remember it in the dragging tap-tap of my grandfather's wooden leg, and in the rough stonework of the war memorial I sat on when the neighbor's kids played all around me, and my legs were hurting.

Even now, many decades on, I often dream of having my legs amputated, the site of my pain vanishing. I imagine it like my grandfather's leg: a blankness, the red-white stump I saw so often. But my grandfather did speak in short sentences of the ghosts, of the leg extending back into his own history, the phantom pains of his amputated limb. My amputation dream often ends on these fantasized moments: me in a watery landscape, bombs, trenches, fire in my nonexisting nerves, endless burning.

In British and Aotearoan/New Zealand hospices, I have worked with elders in the last months of their lives. We write together, dance hand-dances, explore objects like stones and shells from their favorite woods or beaches, remember landscapes no longer accessible to them, and share intensities of life. And I make sure that I mention my nationality early on, when I introduce myself, and I learn to gently bow out when I can see upset spread in a blood tide over a face.

Reclamation

In the reclaiming of the Duin en Bosch asylum site in the dunes, I see no space for survivors, no narratives (yet) that shape how the large institution is remembered. Stephanie and I, travelling tourists wheeling and walking over the site, encounter the nurses' wing, in the process of being rebuilt as a private condo block. A separation into a different kind of nuclear life.

We go up to talk to the workers. The contractor knows nothing about this being an asylum before, part of a huge site dedicated to psychiatric difference. "Nothing like that here. I know nothing. These will be nice private homes." He is belligerent, and we veer off.

The young man who now lives in the guard quarters is much more welcoming. "Yes, this was the police house. That over there, the nurses' quarters. The dorms are behind the trees, and yes, there are still five or six active right now, with many spaces abandoned."

How can asylum space be part of life space if stigma still persists? I try to see all sides to the dunescape, these impermanent markers of lives in abeyance, before entering back (hopefully) into the flow of Dutch life. But the vehemence of the worker irks, sets the needle where it hurts.

Institutions are part of the social contract we have built for ourselves: soldiers and nuns, hospitals and schools, prisons and nursing homes. The *Asylum Project* and its poetic art practices uses its own register to call for change. How can we renegotiate the contract, care in the community, become the kind of social people who help each other interdependently? How can we create moments of apartness, when necessary, without screening them in, in stigma, creating fixed walls? What lands commemorate our dead, and hold up our living?

Asylum[1]

(upon a drifting at the Traverse City State Hospital, Michigan)

The smell of hair, a shirt that holds
compass of someone's arms, endangered

bed becomes mellow ocean
sails toward an invisible edge

"here be monsters"
racket beyond the door, the Cerberus demands
its due on the threshold
the nightingale that sings at the wrong time,
against the beat again, again.
Too soon, the warm gruel
the bedpan tilts,

and the ocean spills into a delta
that holds no body

no hyacinth, no round,
no nightflowering jasmine

no wine-dark seas
no camp, no fire

just the dream of sails, away.
The compass of these arms empty

dragons rise when I dream of your eyes
your tongue turns in my heart
the key drops out of my hands

into Jonah's belly, falls,
an elevator of despair

a knot that won't unfold in the night wind
in the hurricane in the cyclone

that howls on the other side of the door
the gray corridor with its stripes of green and blue

please please let me
let me
just lie here, pillow dolphin
duvet dreams
blood tick
till the 6pm dinner tray and the yogurt cup
stirred, counter-clockwise maelstrom, for luck.

let me
close the door again and dream of arms
outside

Note

1. The poem "Asylum" initially appeared in *White Stag* (2016), and is reprinted in my poetry collection *Gut Botany* (2020). An early version of this essay appeared as "Blood Compost" in *P-Queue* 15 (2018): 43–58.

Works Cited

Conquergood, Dwight. 1985. "Performing as a Moral Act: Ethical Dimensions of the Ethnography of Performance." *Literature in Performance* 2 (5): 1–13.
Haraway, Donna. 2016. *Staying with the Trouble: Making Kin in the Chthulucene*. Durham and London: Duke University Press.
Lai, Larissa. 2002. *Salt Fish Girl*. Toronto: Thomas Allen Publishers.
Onrust, Marjan. 1993. *Waanzin Gevangen (Madness Imprisoned)*. Masters Thesis in Sociology, Univ. of Amsterdam.
Whitman, Walt. 1867. "This Compost!" From *Leaves of Grass*. Available at the Walt Whitman Archive. https://whitmanarchive.org/published/LG/1867/poems/142

Part III

Liminal (Dis)locations

12

A Tide in the River: Auditory Ecologies of Dyarubbin

Nicole Matthews

On the Water

Launching my kayak in the misty hour before sunrise, single-sided deafness gives me direction, a route out and back. I paddle along the left bank of the river, hearing ear tuned to the very beginnings of the dawn chorus. It's still quiet. The jet skiers and the powerboat hoons haven't left their beds yet. There are a few fishermen in tinnies out, putt-putting along. I'm turning a deaf ear to them. It's probably not the safest bet to ignore the sounds of outboard motors—that engine note could be approaching, though I find it hard to tell. But it works for me. I'm holding on to the tranquility of the early morning, making it last.

It's quieter and safer on the river in the early morning. I've been out on the water at the other end of the day, in the golden hour, as the sun's sinking. It's beautiful, too. Late afternoon light on the sandstone escarpments that fall into the creekside mangroves; 180 million years of river sand piled 200 meters high. It's something to see. But I've had more hassle then—Sunday afternoon boaters, blokes in sunnies with their shirts off, boozy and careless. Roaring round river bends too fast and too close, appearing without warning, making waves that toss you in the air. You can tuck your boat close to the rocky shore; it could protect you, but it could also smash you.

N. Matthews (✉)
Macquarie University, Sydney, NSW, Australia
e-mail: nicole.matthews@mq.edu.au

Better to be on the water for sun-up, to watch the day unfurl from its cocoon of mist. The silence is shared with a white-bellied sea eagle. A bold profile in the canopy, looking out for the first rays of light. A crowd of passerines is leaping around in the scrub by the waterside—silvereyes or maybe thornbills. I know they're somewhere nearby, but I have no idea where. I sit very still in the boat, listening hard for peeps and squeaks and scanning for a twitch in the foliage. The falling tide pulls me away. I splash back and listen hard again. Hearing from only one ear, you lose "binaural summation"—the brain's ability to swiftly compare the sounds from two sources to give a sense of distance and position. Instead, to find out where things are, I have to be on the move. Head this way and that. A few steps in one direction, a step or two back. A little way downriver, a little way up, like the tide.

It's such a hearing hobby, bird watching, despite the name. Nearly twenty years of glacially learned sign language have sharpened my peripheral vision, though (Bauman and Murray, 2009, 2014). In the Deaf world, a sudden movement in the corner of your eye could be someone joining the conversation, an interjection, a disagreement, or a joke. Here, it could be a rock warbler, Sydney's only endemic bird, collecting fragments of spiderweb for its nest in a crack in the riverside rocks.

My good camera with the long lens goes out in the kayak with me. It's risky but worth it. The fog simplifies the landscape, blanking out distractions. I pour myself into the distant scene, deep inside the camera—a portrait of a yacht becalmed, mist spilling out of a gully and trickling across the water, the sun white in a gray sky. I stalk the hunting herons and whirling swallows, apparitions in the cloud.

I pick the place to put in my boat with a tide chart. Out with the falling tide, and back on a rising one—that's the best. Down river, into deeper water, as the tide level falls. On my usual trips, it's the left bank that first catches the sun, wakes the birds, warms frozen feet. And back again, lifted by the river, hearing ear to the shore. Going with the flow.

Luckily, my house is perched on a ridge between the sinuous branches of this flooded river valley. I have plenty of beaches and boat ramps to choose from for a favorable tide: car parks full of boat trailers or sleepy byways near the night ferry, colored lights softened by the fog. I started to think about this harbor city differently since I took up paddling a decade ago—noticing not so much its choked thoroughfares and contorted railway lines, but the waterways they skirt around. Here, on the far fringes of the city, the fingers of the river wrap around our town. Way below the freeway, beneath the layer of mist that settles under the cover of darkness, there's water all around us. Held by river, it feels like we're in safe hands.

12 A Tide in the River: Auditory Ecologies of Dyarubbin

We settlers call it "The Hawkesbury River" but, like Sydney Harbour to the south, it's salty. The Quaternary Marine Transgression that drowned the river started 18,000 years ago and went on for another 10,000 years, as the glaciers melted and sea water swelled. Somewhere beneath the surface of the Pacific, wending across what's now the Continental Shelf, you'll find the rest of the river channel. As the planet warmed, the waters rose and rose, and the tide crept further and further up the creeks and gorges, bringing salt, deeper water, oyster beds. It's hard to imagine what it must have been like for the first people here, moving again and again ahead of the rising sea, away from the coastal flat lands to the hills of the Hornsby Plateau, above and around Dyarubbin.

If you look at this waterway on the map or from a plane, it seems like river. It skirts the foothills of the Blue Mountains, running north, winding parallel to the coast, and then swings towards the ocean. Around here, at the boundary of Darkinjung, Darug, and Garigal country, tributaries join it—Mangrove and Mullet Creek, Mooney Mooney and Marramarra, Patonga and Berowra Creek, Cowan Water. A "creek"—sounds like a stream you might leap across on stepping stones, a rivulet tumbling down a hot hillside. A waterway where you could carefully fill up your billy, for an iffy cup of tea. But Dyarubbin and all these creeks and waters are brackish. It's an estuary, with a tidal limit 140 kilometers from the river mouth at Broken Bay.

This valley was carved by fresh water, and now it's something else. Not all flooded river valleys have this mix of salt and sweet water. Sydney Harbour is a truly marine environment—it *is* the sea. Dyarubbin is different. Like me: once one thing, now not quite the other. Somewhere in between.

When rain trickles down the damp gullies in Berowra Creek, it tumbles over sandstone cliffs straight into salty water. Up from the boat ramp, I head into an alleyway between the mangroves to visit one of these waterfalls. There's a way through the half-submerged boulders, even for a breakable wooden boat like mine, to the swimming hole under the overhang. It's a special place: rock orchids up high, ferns tugged by dripping water, the red spiderflowers leaning down to a pool of chilled air.

I follow the streak of an azure kingfisher as it flashes along the mangrove's eaves. There's white noise, a subdued roar, and I wonder if it's the drenching of the last few days finding its way over the cliff. But no, I'm hearing my own internal sounds: tinnitus. I don't wear my hearing aid out on the water (the cost of possibly dropping my camera is quite enough!), so the background hiss is louder here. Sometimes it shifts note, tuning into environmental sounds: rain on the roof, the hum of the fridge, the static of a waterfall. That rushing sound has been my constant companion since the morning I woke up with a "blocked ear" ten years ago. These days it feels like there's something barring the way on my right. A wall? Or perhaps a rock face, with a jumble of sandstone boulders at its foot. My attention, the busy "hearing" part of my brain, pushes against that blockage, pushes past it, making the sound of a ghostly cascade.

On Track

After taking up kayaking, I understand why, in the years before the railway, British merchants built networks of canals to link their ports and mines and factories. Compared to walking, moving through the water is so fast and easy, frictionless. I glide between the banks of the river on a Sunday morning—the same route takes hours and hours on foot on the fire trails that contour the steep wooded slopes above. Even so, I walk the trails often, escaping pandemic lockdowns and long working days with a sunset amble to a lookout. Lucky me—even when we weren't allowed to travel more than a few kilometers from home, I could still find a friend to walk with and a path to follow, on the suburban streets of the shale-topped ridges or to the angophora forest below.

Day-hikers and dog-walkers share these trails with the mountain-bikers. The cyclists explode out of nowhere when they approach on my right. I'm never prepared for them, even though I'm amplified on land. My "cheap" Costco hearing aid makes conversation easier. Still, my differential hearing orients me, gives a kind of handedness to the landscape. One half of the valley to attend to, one half to neglect. My trusted walking companions know which side of the track to keep, how to stay on the right side of me—the left. The wide trails that loop above the river aren't just useful firebreaks and fast routes to a blaze. You can walk side-by-side here—COVID-19-safe, but close enough to keep a conversation going. It's best, I find, to walk to the bush with amateur actors, university lecturers, excitable teenagers, and people who spent their formative years in noisy nightclubs—people who know how to project. A fire trail is good for signing, too—wide enough to walk a comfortable distance apart and to even accommodate my overlarge, "shouty" Australian Sign Language (Auslan).

Conversations on narrow trails are harder. Spinning round to catch a phrase, I might be scratched by the twigs of a mountain devil or stumble on a pathside rock. Brush against the foliage and a grass tick might secretly bury itself in your flesh.

I like the sign in Auslan for communication breakdown. You hold both hands in the shape of a C, palms facing. To sign "communication," each hand moves towards and away from each other, overlapping momentarily and then moving apart, in a plane extending out from your chest. For "communication breakdown," your dominant hand, the one farthest from you, suddenly drops a few centimeters, the way a car would clunk down if a wheel fell off. Both hands stop still. This sign pops into my mind while walking and talking on a little winding trail. It's connected in my head, via the C handshape, with the sign for "van"—one hand moving forward and the other back to smoothly mark the form of a long metal tube with wheels. Conversation on single-track is like talking to someone sitting to the back of you in a van. It's always better to be in front. But I'm often behind.

It's such a familiar feeling, missing words, saying "sorry" (I use it so often, I was given it as my sign name), asking people to repeat themselves again (and again). Someone says, "It doesn't matter" or "I'll tell you later." It's no big deal for me, really. Just everyday annoyance, ordinary irritation, unremarkable interpersonal friction. I'm still (mostly) hearing. In the right environment, I can catch what people are saying. Not like my granddad, who slowly lost sound in his fifties. He could sustain a short chat over a cup of tea and toast. But a few minutes in, he would wander off to his easy chair, sport on TV, volume to the max. When he did leave the house, it was for games of tennis with New Australians, athletic but not so comfortable in English. No need for yabber. The ball passing regularly from one side of the net to the other.

Most sign languages are topic/comment languages. You get the general theme of the utterance first, and then the details. "Walk—where?" Sometimes if you're being asked a question, you get it twice, at the beginning and at the end. I really wish English worked more like this. A word at the start to orient you, to give you direction. And a chance to catch up, important things repeated at the end.

It makes sense that sign languages will show you the way—their grammar is spatial (Sutton-Spence and Woll, 1998; de Beuzeville, Johnston, and Schembri, 2009). If you're telling a story, you set the scene in the space before you. The river is here. Your hand shows the shape of the hill, the direction you're walking in. In the telling, you can see if your companion is tall or short, if they walk in front or beside you, if they're looking towards you or out at the view. A sign has orientation and movement, but also location. You know where you are.

In English (and perhaps in Auslan, too), it's easier for me to talk than listen. If you set the path of the conversation, you know where it's likely to go.

I'm still a hearing person, but places matter to me more than before, especially when I'm walking with someone, talking. How far apart are we on the track? How loud is the wind in the trees? Do our boots crunch on the gravel?

Are the sulphur-crested cockatoos squalling above us in the Sydney red gums, so loud I can't really hear?

Eli Clare says, "white western culture goes to extraordinary lengths to deny the vital relationships between water and stone, plant and animal, human and non-human, as well as the utter reliance of human upon human" (2017, 136). Maybe I'm starting to understand this lesson in connection, the way we become people in place. Dyarubbin and Darug country have been teaching these lessons for a long time, even if we settlers haven't really been learning them.

These days, my blood bears the mark of this landscape. Thanks to those pathside grass ticks, my years in the bush around Dyarubbin have given me an allergy to red meat. Ticks feed on wallabies and bandicoots—more common than before, with the native dingoes gone and the feral foxes baited. Then the ticks feed on people, injecting a sugar—alpha-gal—that sensitizes their immune system (my immune system) to mammal meat. A careless meal or an insect bite can make you sick or even kill you. Odd as it sounds, this allergy isn't uncommon around here in the northern suburbs of Sydney, where suburban gardens bleed into national parks. I take an Epipen with me when I go out these days. Connections to place can be dangerous. Choosing to be a vegetarian as a teenager, long ago, now seems like a strange kind of foresight.

My hearing aid amplifies the cockatoos' screams perfectly. It's almost like it was made for them, tuning exactly to the ripped-paper rawness of their calls. I'm reminded of the complaints of a "ten-pound Pom" on a TV documentary a few years ago. One of the British people who came over to Australia on a ship in the years after the Second World War, she wasn't fond of the local soundscape. Birds in England go "tweet tweet," she said, but the ones in Australia just go "squaaaaak." I'm sure she was thinking of cockies. Needless to say, that Pom went back to the Old Country. But I admire the cockatoos—they're rowdy and destructive, but you can't help but be impressed with them. They mate for life, staying permanently in family groups, and they live a long time—up to sixty years. Sixty years of fighting and shrieking, yellow crests raised in alarm and aggravation. Then sometime later, inching together on a branch to shyly neck and groom. A couple land in the twisted pink branches of the angophora. One starts tearing at the rotten heartwood, scratching away a nesting hollow. The cockatoos can handle friction in their sulphurous romances.

In another strange moment of foresight, a folding of time, I started taking sign-language classes long before my hearing changed for good. I took my first lessons soon after my son died as a one year old. He wasn't deaf, but had he lived, he would for certain have used some alternative form of communication—big buttons, or devices that read your eye gaze, or Makaton. Learning British Sign Language (and later Auslan) seemed a way of marking his life, of deference to a path not taken, respect for other ways of living and being. A beautiful boy, lost suddenly and shockingly—for a beautiful language, gained imperfectly, and painfully slowly: not really an exchange, but some kind of compensation.

Maybe it was also a way of trying to manage the future. Both my dad and my grandfather lost their high-frequency hearing while they were still of working age. My auntie, my mum's sister, had otosclerosis as a young adult, ear bones fused in place, dulling the sound of the world. As long as I can remember, she read lips and wore hearing aids. Having a Plan B seemed sensible. Be prepared for everything.

Deaf people have long resisted the language of "hearing loss." Bauman and Murray note that hearing people see deafness as "an absence, a void, a lack. It is virtually impossible to think of deafness without thinking of loss. And yet Deaf people do not often consider their lives to be defined by loss" (2009, 3). Instead of "hearing loss," they talk about "Deaf gain." The idea can be glossed, they say, by three different signs in American Sign Language: "Deaf increase," "Deaf benefit," and "Deaf contribute." The Auslan sign for Deaf gain contains the sign for "profit"—thumb and forefinger together putting something in your top pocket. A gain for Deaf people and the Deaf community. But I'm sharply aware of "Deaf contribute"—"how Deaf culture can contribute to the general good of humanity" (Bauman and Murray, 2009, 7), of the many ways I've benefited from the patience and generosity of Deaf teachers and friends.

I'm not sure what I have to contribute, in my fall away from clarity. Is there "hard-of-hearing" gain? Certainly nothing especially surprising or beautiful. I'm not one of the "people of the eye," communicating easily through the air with my body and face and hands (Bauman and Murray, 2009). What have I got to offer? Repetition. Some embarrassingly loud talking in public places. Friction and irritation. A little bit of confusion. Certainly anxiety.

But maybe there's something there. A willingness to plunge in first without really knowing where I'm going, taking a guess, taking the lead through the tangle of little paths too close to the cliff tops. And repetition—both friend and foe. I don't mind repeating myself; others often have to repeat themselves to me. In fact, I like it. My Deaf friends are globetrotters, leveraging their visual language and their deftness at bridging communication gaps in the wide world of signers. Over the years, my social world has got smaller—bars and restaurants are too hard, too loud to hear well in. Even with one functional ear, I've lost "binaural squelch," which helps the brain separate speech from ambient noise. Easiest to communicate with a few people at a time. Preferably the shouters.

But a tolerance of repetition and a habit of avoiding crowds has been an asset in Corona times. I don't mind walking the same fire trails, to the same lookouts, to take in the same views over the same creek, again and again. What do you see when you step into the same river, time after time after time? Repetition with minor variation sharpens your eyes to changes in the light or the tide, the movement of mist or ripples or bird flight. A single rower appearing through the fog. Haunted ships swaying gently. Sunrise returning, finding a new path through the same trees.

I imagine what happened to my hearing as topographic. The night before we were in the mountains, for a friend's fiftieth birthday party. We drove home the long way—not the freeway to the city but the narrow switchback road that crossed the river at Yarramundi, at the very limits of Dyarubbin's tidal range. It's always been an important meeting and trading place for First Nations people. The road goes on through Windsor, a town built on the rich alluvial soil that was the site of some of the bloodiest battles of the long frontier war between European colonists and the Darug people.

As we came down the mountain, the pressure built up and never really lifted, not with nose blowing in the shower, or antibiotics, or, much later, high-dose steroids that made me hysterically weepy and constipated, but did nothing for my high-frequency hearing. I was sent home from my Auslan night classes, giddy and a little sick, and went back the next week with single-sided hearing. Deep inside my cochlea, something had shifted.

Then a few years later, as I came down the long slope from Anaiwan and Kamilaroi lands on the Thunderbolts Way, driving off the Great Dividing Range—the old mountains that follow the east coast all the way to the tropics—it happened again. Inside the mysterious labyrinth of the ear, something tectonic had taken place, and now, with just a little pressure, things crack and crumble, falling into a new position. I have a prescription for those corticosteroids sitting on my sideboard, to start immediately if, on some other mountainous road trip, something slips away again. Sudden hearing loss is a medical emergency, they say. I'm not so sure. I'm not sure I'll take them.

I had a strange sense of satisfaction when I got my diagnosis. The audiologist and the student sitting in expected an uneventful hearing test, I think, or as the appointment wore on, perhaps a middle-ear infection. They looked more and more troubled as each new measuring device was wheeled in. At the end of the appointment, the audiologist told me, with a serious look on her face, that I had sensory-neural hearing loss. There was nothing to be done about it. No fix, just workarounds. She expected me to be upset—in fact, I was buoyant. After six months of wondering if I was imagining things, thinking I might be making too much of it, this was validation. I thought something had changed and I was right. A familiar feeling if you're paying attention in the Anthropocene.

The mob of cockatoos settles in for the night. Screeching, they tumble around above our heads, lifting and landing, meeting and parting. Then, one by one, little family groups take off over the treetops, high above the still water of the creek. I know where they're heading—two huge Sydney red gums down on the waterline, where they all seem to roost. It's not a one-way process—some pause, fly back, then cross again. They're so loud I can hear their calls retreat into the distance. 3D hearing—something strange and special. Their crisp white wings against the dimming haze of the bush, their faraway voices, stitch the valley together.

On a Rising Tide

I'm paddling upstream, to the navigable limits of Berowra Creek. Under the power lines, either side of the railway, we're in lyrebird country. Superb lyrebirds, famous mimics of everything found in their territory; birdsongs but also car alarms, chainsaws, and shutter clicks haunt these shady valleys. You can usually tell when a call is a lyrebird performance—it's accurate, just a bit too loud. And the sounds of all those many and varied birds—and the car alarm—come from the very same place in the undergrowth. And then the performer emerges from the bushes, singing to itself and scratching at the forest floor. Difficult to miss. Perfect for the hard-of-hearing birdwatcher.

On a paddle not far from here, I heard a lyrebird's mélange of calls—of whipbirds and kookaburras, bowerbirds and currawongs. But in among these birds of the leaf litter and the gum trees, a sound I'd never heard a lyrebird make before: that paradigmatic bird of the beach—the silver gull. That's the soundtrack of this flooded river valley, right there. A climate catastrophe long ago, that brought salt water to the foot of the rainforest, embedded in a mimic's song.

You can see as well as hear the past, paddling up this creek. Everywhere you look are midden heaps, meters high. The bushwalking tracks pass over them, excavating bone-white shell flakes that spill down the slopes. It feels wrong to walk there. From the water, you see the layers of mussel and oyster fragments, held in place by the grasses, woven through the roots of the she-oaks. Thousands of years of campfire meals: this is a landscape long known, long cared for, as Darug Ngurra tells us (2021). Even after the colonists arrived in places like this, First Nations people survived on country. As Jodi Frawley says, "the wetlands and estuaries were refuges precisely because settlers saw them as wastelands" (2020, 180).

There are so many middens, but so few oysters these days. The shellfish didn't just grow here: the custodians of these waters cultivated them, for millennia, throwing spent shells back into the water, making a hard substrate where oyster sprat could grow. The river bottom is sandy now.

There's a scraping sound. I worry it's the delicate hull of my craft, scratching across the riverbed. I look around to read the water and the noise returns. Then I realize what I'm hearing is just the brim of my hat rasping on my lifejacket. I think about edges and boundaries—of my body, this boat, the river. The way your senses catch, rub against those edges, are held inside those boundaries, or move out far beyond them. Sometimes the canoe is like a resonance chamber. I swear I *feel* the shallows: a pressure-wave of displaced water bouncing off the bottom and pushing back against the skin of the canoe.

Berowra Creek was deeper once, before the felling for the housing estates further up in the catchment. Sharks swam around the car ferry, they say. Then the silt washed down and lined the creek—if you make the mistake of paddling upstream at low tide, you'll have to get out and walk. Carefully, because there's seagrass here and sometimes, snuggled into the soft mud, stingrays.

It's tempting to think of this—silt accruing, mangroves encroaching onto clear water—as a retreat from the natural way of the river. But there's no easy foothold for the "natural" in a flooded river valley. The water was deeper here before, one hundred years and 120,000 years ago. When they built the new railway bridge over Dyarubbin, at Brooklyn, during the War, they dug the footings into the mud, 180 feet below the high waterline—and still couldn't find bedrock. As I paddle, like Eli Clare, I'm thinking "about natural and unnatural, trying to grasp their meanings. . . . What was once normal here; what can we consider normal now?" (2017, 16).

I'm away upriver on a rising tide, one of many to come. The water's moving higher again, not so fast as the Quaternary perhaps, but lifting sea levels are locked in now. There's no fix for this, just workarounds. Of course, the people who lived here 10,000 years ago, who live here still, have seen it all happen before. Little comfort to Dyarubbin's settler river towns, drowned three times in two years. Two years of La Niña with record-breaking downpours. Once-in-a-century floods now coming two, three times a year. Down on the plains, the brown water of Dyarubbin rising above its banks, the bridges, the roofs of the houses, again and again.

Even here, up on the plateau, relentless rain has softened the sandy soil, crept into the cracks. The hairpinned road that crosses the gorge upstream,

12 A Tide in the River: Auditory Ecologies of Dyarubbin

often blocked by impetuous truck drivers or lost gray nomads, is shut now, for at least three months, by a landslip. Rocks and soil spilling out across the tarmac. Everything shifting, going downhill.

You can still get there on Berowra Creek in a boat, among the debris. This is one of Dyarubbin's murkier waterways, with sewage outflows, runoff, and weeds. Certainly no wilderness. My suburban adventures could never be framed as a triumphant overcoming of unforgiving nature, even though, on the water at dawn, you could be in the middle of nowhere. There's a hint of "civilization" as you pass the scout camp and the rundown convention center and catch the smell of breakfast bacon, and then you're back in the fog and the towering eucalypts.

A rising tide brings sea water—clearer, bottle green. On the other side of the railway line, in more oceanic reaches, I'm wary of looking down into the vertiginous depths. You can see right through the mirrored surface your fragile vessel is floating on, far below to another, verdigris world. My ENT told me not to go scuba diving. Water pressure down there might be too much for my "good" ear. A Deaf friend I've been meeting for lunch and Auslan chat for over a decade says, "You're prepared, go for it!" Plunge in and see it close up, a place where sign language works perfectly and speech not at all. If it's all too much for your ears, it will be no disaster.

I have met people, though, for whom suddenly losing their hearing was a catastrophe, at least at first. Middle-aged teachers, social workers—professional talkers—drowning after suddenly falling into a silent world where they have no functional language. When I met them—at sign language intensives, deeply immersed in a new way of living—they were saving themselves. But, for the moment, they were still at sea.

Risky as it is, Alison Kafer thinks that we should acknowledge these losses: sensory, embodied, ecological. She remembers, before her injuries, the solitary pleasures of running—on the beach, through the woods—and mourns how hard it is, now that she uses a wheelchair, to get to the hilltops or the waterline (Kafer, 2017). If, one day, the rest of my hearing is demolished in another roadtrip rockfall, my visits to this place—the cryptic little birds in the canopy quietened—won't be the same. When I came up this creek at the height of summer cicada season, the wall of noise pounding from the riverside trees was so intense I plugged my hearing ear to protect it. I'm not sure what to make of this—dangers and pleasures, losses and joys, mixed together like saltwater and sweet.

Perhaps there is something to be learned from a flooded valley, a river that reaches out below the ocean and pulses with salt one hundred miles from the shore. Lessons of living with change: of knowing what can't be halted, knowing the tides to ride and the floods to run from, of being betwixt and between.

The top of the creek is a Japanese garden: boulders, carefully placed, patched with lichen and moss, ferns growing in the shadows of vines and the gentle sound of tumbling water. Even the weeds here, washed down from the yards of unwise gardeners, flower decorously. If you pull your boat in, you can walk beyond the rocky rubble to the water-carved pools of Fish Ponds. But this is as far as I can go on the creek. For now. I know, though, in the unmanageable future that we've made for ourselves, this place will go under. Awful. Unthinkable.

But I think of it: new reaches of water; a wooden kayak floating above the sandstone; being lifted beyond the cascade. You paddle around the next loop of the river, and the sounds of the waterfall are abruptly silenced. The still green water shimmers ahead.

Works Cited

Bauman, H-Dirksen L., and Joseph J. Murray. 2009. "Reframing: From Hearing Loss to Deaf Gain." *Deaf Studies Digital Journal* 1: 1–10.

Bauman, H-Dirksen L., and Joseph J. Murray, eds. 2014. *Deaf Gain: Raising the Stakes for Human Diversity*. Minneapolis: University of Minnesota Press.

de Beuzeville, Louise, Trevor Johnston, and Adam Schembri. 2009. "The Use of Space with Indicating Verbs in Auslan: A Corpus-based Investigation." *Sign Language & Linguistics* 12 (1): 53–82.

Clare, Eli. 2017. *Brilliant Imperfection: Grappling with Cure*. Durham, NC: Duke University Press.

Frawley, Jodi. 2020. "Adapting to Change in Australian Estuaries: Oysters in the Techno-Fix Cycles of Colonial Capitalism." In *Environments of Empire: Networks and Agents of Ecological Change*, ed. Ulrike Kirchberger and Brett M. Bennett, 176–194. Chapel Hill: University of North Carolina Press.

Kafer, Alison. 2017. "Bodies of Nature: The Environmental Politics of Disability." In *Disability Studies and the Environmental Humanities: Toward an Eco-Crip Theory*, ed. Sarah Jaquette Ray and Jay Sibara, 201–241. Lincoln: Univ. of Nebraska Press.

Ngurra, Darug, Lexodious Dadd, Corina Norman-Dadd, Marnie Graham, Sandie Suchet-Pearson, Paul Glass, Rebecca Scott, Harriet Narwal, and Jessica Lemire. 2021. "Buran Nalgarra: An Indigenous-led Model for Walking with Good Spirit and Learning Together on Darug Ngurra." *AlterNative* 17 (3): 357–367.

Sutton-Spence, Rachel, and Bencie Woll. 1998. *The Linguistics of British Sign Language*. Cambridge: Cambridge University Press.

13

Hydra, New Hampshire

Stephen Kuusisto

This is a story about place, but it's also about the kids in the grass. All of us played at living and dying in tall grass. We tore our clothes in grass; scraped skin from our arms; slapped at midges and mosquitoes. Sometimes we pressed our mouths into green and sucked moisture—though one of us, an older one (that knowing child found in every group)—said the earth was radioactive, and we believed her because she said President Kennedy said it. We were clear-headed by turns, then knocked flat. There were, we knew, monsters beyond the grass. We played by following it. Following grass. The times were plain. Some of us knew the names of birds. My favorite was the white-throated sparrow, whom we called the "Peabody bird." His little song could break your heart. Lots of things could break your heart. The wood thrush was also a heartbreaker, and he'd get inside us when we were lying face down in the woods. He'd get inside us because we were playing dead. This was in the final days before television. We played dead and listened to bird songs.

* * *

I was the blind kid uncoiling in light, who ran just as fast as he could. That was a job for me. It was "the" job. I'd run a zig-zag staggering lurching tear-soaked gambol, while others threw pinecones and pebbles at my back and

S. Kuusisto (✉)
Syracuse University, Syracuse, NY, USA
e-mail: sakuusis@syr.edu

legs. I was the "Kraut." The crippled kid was always the Kraut. Once, a rock struck the back of my skull—not quite errant (there was too much laughter) and not lethal, not enough to run to mommy—but I was thoroughly admonished to be dead, and so I lay down. Nice and easy. Beyond the grass stirred uncertainties, especially if you couldn't see. Be foreign. Notice how the clover smells like hay. Listen to cornstalks beside a rail fence. Think about the darkness and sadness of joy because you're blind and still. Think, though you're scarcely eight, about the coppery gleam of names because you've been called too many for such a small boy—*blindo, Mr. Magoo, four eyes, froggo,* and *freak of nature*, which later you will learn in Latin. *Lusus* is monster. In high school, you'll think of writing a play called *Lusus-stratus*, though you won't. By the time you're in your teens, you'll have other blue mantles.

But childhood grass was democracy. Each of us played war and smiled the faintly sardonic smile of outcasts. Perhaps we were all chameleons hoping to be changed. For a time, though, for that time, we kept to the grasses and weeds. But I was the only one whose blood-red-thickened name followed him as he crawled like a soldier. Blind snake.

* * *

Home again, he listened to long-playing records on a government gramophone for the blind.

It was a hot, lonesome Sunday. He absorbed words read aloud from a long-playing record.

Hercules fought a nine-headed snake. The needle quavered, struck at the paper label. He turned the thing over.

What were a blind child's eyes worth? The answer: one name of the Hydra.

* * *

Snakes were half-stone, half-grass.

Some lived under the pond. Of course, they couldn't see.

Within her nine heads, all fanged, nine kinds of love.

No wonder he grew to love Hydra.

All she wanted was a lithic solitude.

* * *

A neighbor—an attorney—went to the meadow with a gun.

He was going to demonstrate heroism by shooting snakes.

When he was out of sight, the boys taunted me.

"You can't come because you're blind!"

"Yeah, you might get hurt!"

A pinecone struck me in the chest.

"Look! He didn't even see that coming!"

"A snake might bite him!"

Then they were gone.

* * *

Hydra, I took you under my ribs, my darling who licked the words from stones.

Hydra, my speechlessness.

* * *

In the grass, he wore fear, a homespun shirt. He raised the emerald spindrift in mind. He saw if you became the green, you would not have need of it.

If the grass was democratic, it was owing to unspeakable loneliness. Hydra. Long and low and still.

* * *

When he was grown, he remembered other boys and girls who held themselves perfectly still in the green unspoken.

He found it difficult to tell the story of grass and the aspen that shivered and the names inside him.

Hydra was a reconciliation of what was practical.

Now he calls her the nine-times-multiplied name of children who expect they'll die. For whom it started as a game.

He supposed he should be more ironic about fealty and Romantic sadness, but finds he cannot.

He's still there in rain and green, listening.

Even a child knows Hydra is formally incomplete.

* * *

One day I climbed the tallest tree in Durham, New Hampshire, and by God, I felt richly alive up there where the leaves were all so close and you could hear the wind.

Hydra: I climbed many trees after that. Up and up. I could feel the earth trembling slightly, pure, roots, breezes, a full moon. Hydra. We lived in a place and time without Heracles. We flew. Rested. Lay still. Or simply listened to the deep-voiced stars.

14

Between Places

Leigh A. Neithardt

I have fallen so many times in my life that I now rank and categorize each fall. Most embarrassing tumble? Into the river at a state park on the sixth-grade field trip. One of the teachers had to come in after me after I'd insisted on traversing the big log across the river by myself. Most painful? Slipping on black ice after getting off the bus near my apartment in Columbus, Ohio. I was surprised by my sudden change of direction. I fell hard and fast and lay on the ground, unable to breathe (or so it seemed), my left arm and both knees throbbing. I managed to hobble home and sat with my legs up for the next several hours, unable to move without the pain intensifying. Most terrifying of all? Tripping over my own foot (I think) on the back stairs of my sister's house three years ago. I watched the concrete ledge that ran along the wall rise to meet me, certain I was in for a head or neck injury. I closed my eyes, threw myself backward toward the wall, and managed to stand upright. The only damage was a webbed crack in the wall where my right foot made contact.

I was born with cerebral palsy (CP), so my balance and coordination have always been questionable at best. If it is possible to fall somewhere, I've probably done it, or eventually will. Trains, boats, open fields, gravel driveways, sidewalks, streets, carpet, tile, up stairs, down stairs. I've stumbled on a beach in Israel. I've slipped and slid down a muddy hill in Costa Rica. My favorite surfaces are flat, dry, unmoving. I need level ground that I can see completely

L. A. Neithardt (✉)
Modern Language Association, New York, NY, USA
e-mail: leigh.neithardt@gmail.com

across at once. If I can't see the entire lay of the land, then I have to figure out which route will be the least painful if I fall. Consigning myself to a fall ahead of time means embracing helplessness. It means almost constant planning for injury and pain—though I'm simply trying to move from Point A to Point B. I engage in this unnerving calculus most often in the winter. Iced-over, hard snow; black ice; regular old clear ice—all are unintended but consequential enemies. Of course, they only cause me trouble because people haven't cleared them properly.

This thoughtlessness or laziness is magnified by the frustration that, most often, what is causing trouble is a very small patch of ice or frozen snow. A few square feet, even inches. In the spring, such a patch would not even register as I walk. But in the winter, that same small area of sidewalk or parking lot, that "between place," is suddenly impassable, and might as well be the size of a lake. With reference to Jos Boys's 2014 book, *Doing Disability Differently: An Alternative Handbook on Architecture, Dis/ability and Designing for Everyday Life*, Margaret Price explains:

> [E]ven when aspects of physical access are carefully accounted for, other forms of access, including those that may be more difficult to discern, remain unexplored. These other forms of access may be more difficult to discern because we are accustomed to thinking of access barriers as recognizable, stable entities. But this misses the fact that many barriers—as well as forms of access—arise *in context*, shifting as the circumstances and bodyminds of/in a space shift. (2017, 160)

My CP hasn't advanced or changed; there are no "seasonal" types of CP that one cycles through over the course of a year. What has changed is the landscape following the changes of seasons, and people's understanding about their responsibility to it—and to the people who cross it.

Jay Dolmage writes of people's consideration of space, "[W]e need to care about space. To begin with, we do 'think' spatially—we readily see the world in terms of physical space and spatial relations. … Spaces, and how we write about them, think about them and move through them, suggest and delimit attitudes" (2017, 102–103). Assuming that most of the people who don't always carefully clean the icy, snowy spaces that they're responsible for are able-bodied, they're likely not imagining the disabled people who might also use those places. They're not thinking that such spaces could be occupied at any point by a disabled person, nor about disabled people moving through them. While many nondisabled people are aware that disabled people are no longer on the margins, it seems that we remain theoretical rather than actual.

We are "here," certainly, but not in a specific *here*. "In society," yes, but not in one's parking lot or building—not on one's sidewalk or driveway.

Nor do nondisabled people always fully imagine what the transitional place that enables a disabled person to enter a space should look like. A web search for "accessibility fails" offers pages of frustrating images: elevators that are located up one or two steps; ramps that are too steep or too narrow or that inexplicably end in stairs. These are just a couple of examples of "solutions" that any disabled person would regard with frustration and confusion. Jos Boys writes about the need for architects whose designs consider the bodies of disabled people:

> There are also already a multitude of ways in which architects diagram human occupation. For example, this may be through mapping personal and organizational needs, through articulating our sensory and experiential relationships to built space, and/or through analysing and extrapolating from the patterns of events and flow that we create en masse. Yet in almost every case bodies are assumed mobile, autonomous and with fully working senses (2017, 148).

As a disabled person outside in the winter, I often encounter trouble in "between places" like the narrow area between a street and a sidewalk, bus shelter, or parking lot. These relatively innocuous spaces receive little if any consideration from the people responsible for maintaining them. They assume that the bodies in them will be, in Boys's words, "mobile, autonomous and with fully working senses." The unspoken assumption seems to be this: if you are outside and able to be in one space, then surely you can move from that space into another.

Writing about "Keeping your balance," Boys offers the following "examples of personal, social, material and spatial intersections": "Gravity. Slippery and uneven surfaces. Confusing reflections. Carrying or pushing loads. Scanning for things to hold onto. Dealing with exhaustion and weakness." She contrasts these with various "social norms about space": "Assumption of uninterrupted and fast motion, autonomous, independent and unimpeded by others or by built surroundings" (148). It sounds strange to most people that a few inches or feet could be impossible to navigate, but I have spastic diplegia. It affects my legs, leaving my muscles very tight if I don't exercise to stretch them. Add that to the overall balance and coordination difficulties that I face, and trying to walk easily and safely after a snow or ice storm becomes a challenge. I am likely to get stuck in a between place.

Three Stories of Getting Stuck

1.

One evening in the winter of 2005, I got off the bus across the street from my apartment in northern Virginia and nearly fell. The sidewalk hadn't been fully cleared, and snow had built up and frozen over. I tried to place my feet in the large divots created by others who had stepped off the bus before me, hoping that the holes would be flat and less icy on the bottom so that I could stand firmly. The driver waited for me to get my bearings before leaving. I turned around slowly, looked toward the island in the middle of the street, and then realized that I was stuck. I could pick up my feet, but there was a stretch of frozen snow between me and the street. And the island—which had a sidewalk cutting across it—wasn't cleaned. I squinted and looked at the sidewalk on the far side of the street. Because it unrolled past the end of a cul-de-sac where there were no houses, no one had cleared it either. I paused and wondered what might happen if I made it into the street but fell. Would I be able to get out of the way of a passing car? And then make it across the island and onto the uncleared sidewalk? My legs suddenly began to burn, a signal to my panicking brain that I was standing too rigidly in an attempt to keep myself upright. I felt a tremor begin in my feet and work upward toward my hips. Even though I hadn't moved, I was only a minute or two from falling over.

I turned back around and saw that the sidewalk near the bus stop had been cleared a bit, and the snow wasn't too high. I figured that I could step out of the divots, reach the sidewalk, then wait a half hour for the next bus. I could ride this second bus the final twenty minutes of the route (away from my apartment complex), wait another ten minutes, then take it back down the same road, but in the opposite direction. This would leave me in front of my apartment complex, where the maintenance staff had cleaned the sidewalk. When the bus arrived, the driver came down the steps and stretched out his hand so I could cross those few inches of icy snow that had trapped me in a between place.

Riding the bus past my stop to the end of the route and back again became part of my routine during the winter. Sometimes I'd take a different Metrorail train to the bus stop at the end of the route and get on the bus there. My out-of-the-way travels were always the result of able-bodied people who don't imagine different kinds of bodies moving into, across, and out of a specific space. There are exceptions, of course; every so often, I would ride to the bus stop with the intent of going past it, and then see that someone had cleared the sidewalk, the path across the island, and the unclaimed sidewalk that abutted the cul-de-sac. More than once, my eyes welled with tears of gratitude. Though I never did cry, I always wanted to discover the identity of the conscientious sidewalk clearer, so that I could bake cookies and offer a sincere "thank you."

2.

A few years later, I moved to Columbus, Ohio, to attend school. I looked forward to living in a part of the country where communities would be adept at clearing snow and ice; after all, I told myself, Columbus is in the Midwest, which receives its fair share of snowstorms. I was quickly disabused of this assumption. In the first winter, sheets of ice covered the parking lot of my complex, and parking spaces were outlined by thin mountain ranges of ice that I couldn't step over. The only place where I could guarantee that sidewalks and other walking routes would be completely clear was on campus, and I was fairly certain the only reason for that was a group of university lawyers sitting in a board room somewhere, insisting that it be done to insure against lawsuits.

I lived a block and a half off of a five-lane road that I had to cross to catch a bus to campus. This was a precarious endeavor in any season, because Columbus is not a pedestrian-friendly city. Sidewalks aren't inevitable, so drivers behave as though a person standing on the edge of a street is an aberration, even if crosswalks and walk signs signal the *possibility* of pedestrians who might want to cross an intersection safely. When it snowed, the trek to the nearest crosswalk was dicey, to say the least, because the absence of sidewalks meant I had to walk *in* the street—a street typically not cleared very well. The shortest route to the bus stop was across the five-lane road where it formed a T with the street that led to my apartment.

One afternoon, as I neared the corner, I realized that no one had shoveled the two-foot square of concrete between the street and the bus stop. Because of the recent snow, there was a snowbank along the street about thigh high— thanks to the plow that had cleared the way down to the macadam. Bad news for anyone headed over to the bus stop.

Dawdling is out of the question if you're trying to cross a busy five-lane road in a non-pedestrian-friendly city in the middle of February. I could use the crosswalk a half a block away, but that posed its own set of challenges. No, I'd have to cross here. Yet that meant kneeling on the snowbank to quash it. There was no way I could climb onto and over it; the pile was far too high for me to step on (my legs would have balked at the required stretch); and even if

I managed such a feat, then I'd almost certainly lose my balance and fall backward into the street.

I waited for the perfect slowdown in traffic to make my move. The traffic on any weekday afternoon in Columbus was thick, and these five lanes would never be clear at once. I'd have to act when the three lanes closest to me were empty, and hope that anyone driving in the opposite direction would slow down and allow me to cross. It was fairly easy to cross that day, to my surprise, thanks to kind drivers who stopped for me. But the few people bundled up at the bus stop looked away when they saw me kneel on the snowbank, then use a metal bench to steady myself as I stood. My khaki pants were filthy and soaked from the knees down.

For the first time in my life, I was reduced to crawling on public property, despite being in my thirties and able to walk reasonably well most of the time. I was a little ashamed of myself for having to do it—but even more, I was angry. Why had everyone turned away? Did they assume I didn't want to be seen? But I didn't care who saw me. Was I ridiculous to them, a grown woman kneeling on a snowbank—another Columbus aberration? I've wondered in the years since whether any of them were more deliberate in their snow-and-ice clearing after that. I'm not here in a disabled body to be anyone's lesson in common sense and compassion. But if they went home and did a better job salting and shoveling the next time, maybe they made it easier for someone else to negotiate the sidewalks and parking lots of their neighborhoods.

3.

My tiny town in northern New Jersey is well served by public transportation, and I'm fortunate to have a train station nearby. It's a six-minute walk from my apartment door through the complex, across a brook via a footbridge, and into a parking lot that slopes up to the sidewalk and street. There's a set of stairs for anyone who'd rather not mount the incline. The street isn't a busy one; I rarely have to wait for a car to pass before walking across the road. The edge of the station's property is marked by a curb and a stretch of macadam that rises in a slight incline to the lot. Railroad ties demarcate the end of sparking spots. A fence separates the parking lot from the tracks, with a small break in it next to a flashing sign, and it normally takes me half a minute, once I cross the street, to reach the parking lot and cross the tracks. An easy walk (even when I'm tired) and mostly flat. I take the stairs out of the apartment-complex lot if I'm tired, and then I walk up the part of the incline with the shallowest slope.

One morning in December of 2019, I realized I was going to have a problem. It had snowed the day before, and overnight, all the snow pushed to the curb by the town plow had developed an icy cap: my nemesis. The station lot had been plowed (of course), so commuters could easily park, but the incline up to the lot had not been (of course). Why bother about a space not utilized by cars? I had a few minutes before the train was scheduled to arrive, but not enough time to get to the parking lot's vehicle entrance—and even there, I might get stuck navigating a large patch of ice, since tire treads handle ice better than the treads of my sneakers. I swore under my breath and looked for a spot that had the least amount of snow pushed to the curb; the least amount of snow on the other side of the curb; the shallowest incline into the lot (also covered by the least amount of snow); and the closest proximity to a parking spot sufficiently plowed for me to walk through and get across the tracks. Returning in the dark was even more precarious. I walked the length of the parking lot to the entrance, which was blotchy with black ice; I turned around and walked back to where I'd begun. The safest way to make this journey was to start moving and not stop, because if I did, I could lose my balance on the frozen snow. I had to hope that the spot I'd crossed in the morning would be safe to cross in reverse.

I was lucky *that* night. Then I discovered that my neighbor Joe was often on the same train. The first time he saw me trying to figure out how to get safely out of the station lot, he offered me his hand. This became part of our nightly routine, and I was always glad to see him waiting for me. But as grateful as I was for Joe, I was annoyed that I had to rely on luck and an acquaintance to walk a few steps at most. Why doesn't it occur to anyone to clear a path out of the lot for all the local residents who use the station? I have to think I'm not the only person who finds it difficult to navigate frozen snow—though in a place occupied by more able-bodied people than not, of course, it doesn't surprise me at all that I and others like me are simply unimagined.

Writing about issues of access, Tanya Titchkosky describes the "unimagined": "Many physical and social environments are set up as if they never imagined the incredible variety of bodies, minds, senses, emotions, and lives that are 'us.' Daily life seems instead to function with a mythical, singular conception of the typical human" (2011, 26). It's strange to think that I'm a member of a group of people who go "unimagined" by others. A few weeks ago, I was explaining to a good friend the problem of getting stuck on a sidewalk when one neighbor decides to shovel their sidewalk (thank you!), while the one next door does not, or when they both shovel *their* sidewalks, but refuse to attend to the few inches of sidewalk where their properties meet. "And I get stuck because of two damn inches of unshoveled sidewalk!"

My friend listened quietly while I told this story, and he was silent when I finished. I worried that I'd lost him, that I'd sounded ridiculous for getting upset about such a small area of unshoveled sidewalk. But then he said, "I'd never thought about that before," his voice tinged with wonder and sadness rather than confusion. He was realizing in that moment something that had never occurred to him, something that likely *wouldn't* have occurred to him if I'd not said a word, or if he'd never witnessed me or anyone else having to cope with that "between place." It was something he wished he'd thought of sooner.

In his introduction to *Life As We Know It: A Father, a Family, and an Exceptional Child*, Michael Bérubé argues for the importance of imagining others:

> [It] is part of my purpose, in writing this book, to represent Jamie as best I can—just as it is part of my purpose, in representing Jamie, to ask about our obligations to each other, individually and socially, and about our capacity to imagine other people. I cannot say why it is that we possess the capacity to imagine others, let alone the capacity to imagine that we might have *obligations* to others; nor do I know why, if we possess such things, we so habitually act as if we do not. But I do know that Jamie has compelled me to ask these questions anew, just as I know how crucial it is that we collectively cultivate our capacities to imagine our obligations to each other. (1998, xix)

More than twenty years later, Bérubé's questions about our abilities to imagine others and our obligations to them, his observation that we tend to behave as though we don't have such abilities or obligations, still resonate. Disabled people would experience far fewer instances of getting stuck—or injured—as we move through a world that supposedly welcomes us if more people took the time to imagine us, even when we aren't present. Knowing, of course, that we are—and always will be—here.

Works Cited

Bérubé, Michael. 1998. *Life as We Know It: A Father, a Family, and an Exceptional Child*. New York: Vintage Books.

Boys, Jos. 2017. *Disability, Space, Architecture: A Reader*. E-book ed. New York: Routledge.

———. 2017. "Diagramming For a Dis/ordinary Architecture." In Boys, 135–54.

Dolmage, Jay. 2017. "From Steep Steps to Retrofit to Universal Design, From Collapse to Austerity: Neo-liberal Spaces of Disability." In Boys, 102–13.

Price, Margaret. 2017. "Un/shared Space: The Dilemma of Inclusive Architecture." In Boys, 155–72.

Titchkosky, Tanya. 2011. *The Question of Access: Disability, Space, Meaning*. University of Toronto Press.

15

The Lie of the Land

Annmaree Watharow

My favorite poem in high school was Kenneth Slessor's "Five Bells" (1939), about his friend, cartoonist Joe Lynch, who has too much to drink—maybe—but falls off a passenger ferry in Sydney Harbour—definitely. The poem's speaker famously imagines Lynch looking up into uncertain shapes while drowning. The lines "Deep and dissolving verticals of light / Ferry the falls of moonshine down" speak eloquently to me. Being deafblind is akin to being underwater, looking into the shadowy reaches of the world above, hearing little, everything a blur—the Harbour Bridge a hoary gray haze, the Sydney Opera House pale and unshaped.

In 1973, John Olsen painted a famous mural, *Salute to Five Bells*, which presides over a long, curved wall of the Sydney Opera House. Death stalks this beauty from chthonic depths, as Olsen's creation faces the exact point on the harbor where Lynch drowned on May 14, 1927. Part of the mural imagines images on Lynch's retina to suggest the interesting but fallacious idea that a dying person's eye captures the last things they see.

My brain (like that of many with low vision) fabricates images purportedly from my retina, and in my last-gasp attempt to pretend my sight is not failing, I see a few things that are not there. The most common apparition is one that I call the Phantasm of Pearl Parade. Pearl Beach is a cherished coastal escape

---

A. Watharow (✉)
Centre for Disability Research and Policy at the University of Sydney, Sydney, NSW, Australia
e-mail: annmaree.watharow@sydney.edu.au

from city life—but not from hallucinations. I first saw him decades ago in Missenden Road near Sydney University, where I studied. The non-existent man wears a suit, skulks about in dim, dark spaces, and jumps out at me in various places—Pearl Beach around dusk, a doorway at work, subdued streets, shadowy ferry boats that plow the distance from Circular Quay to Manly. He is keen on seductive restaurant lighting and dim bathrooms with stuttering globes. The phantasm is here, there, and everywhere—an unpredictable jack-in-the-box. Of course, he isn't real. But he wears a fine suit with brass buttons and a burgundy tie. His face is indistinct, almost pixelated. So much detail, yet so illusory.

It's not enough to know that he is the product of my brain confabulating what the retina does not see, because the startle of him jumping out at me is palpable, the adrenaline fright-and-flight response physiological. Gets me every time.

Phantasmic experiences, or visual hallucinations, are not uncommon in those losing sight, but they're not well documented or understood. Hallucinations may be of people, objects, patterns, lights, and landscapes. Sometimes I see palm trees where there are none—like in my bedroom or on a busy city street. These don't startle me, but they were most confusing at first.

The eighteenth-century Swiss scientist Charles Bonnet gives his name to the syndrome combining low vision, intact cognition, and visual hallucinations. Bonnet's grandfather, Charles Lullin, kept a diary of illusory images he encountered when going blind. And so, too, in the last years of his life, Bonnet witnessed the unreal as he experienced vision loss. Charles Bonnet syndrome makes orienteering spaces you can't see fraught and unpredictable. The mind and land can lie.

* * *

Deafblindness results in disorienting consequences (not just the odd hallucination). Our relationships with the world become splintered and unsteady. The place where one has lived a whole life can become a foreign country—the most beautiful coastal city in the world altered when senses are lost, disembodying us from what is known and loved.

Deafblindness is a unique and distinct disability in which neither sense can compensate for the other, something significantly more debilitating and complex than just adding hearing-loss devices supplemented with low-vision supports. More than additive: multiplicative. Sometimes called dual sensory impairment, deafblindness is a complicated kraken—a time-consuming, energy-draining, activity-limiting, participation-reducing condition in which information is received in fragments.

Touch becomes central as a conduit for communication, access to information, and mobility. Communication technology, assistive devices, interpreters, communication guides, and adaptations to the environment may be required for safe navigation of life's terrains. Human assistance is critical. Living with sight and hearing loss necessitates that we depend on both the kindness and skills of others.

I can hear you say: "Sounds awful, but it's uncommon, right?" Yes and no. Congenital deafblindness is rare, but as we age, hearing loss and low vision as single and dual impairments become more prevalent. A quarter of the population experiences significant combined hearing and sight loss by age eighty. Most people won't call themselves disabled or deafblind. They'll just think: "Can't hear very well, don't see too good. I'm getting old!" And here in Australia, First Nations people have sensory losses in high numbers and at earlier ages, though much of it is treatable or preventable.

I, however, have Usher syndrome, which is an inherited combination of congenital hearing loss with an acquired, progressive diminution of sight beginning in the first or second decade of life. Half of the people under sixty-five with deafblindness have Usher syndrome. Diagnosis used to be delayed until the vision loss impinged on activities of daily living or was the cause of accidental injury. In recent years, newborn hearing screening and subsequent genetic testing mean that a diagnosis may occur in babyhood. It's choppy waters for parents who have a child with hearing loss, knowing that their child will also eventually lose vision.

In my case, I was hearing-aided and speech-therapied as a child and then diagnosed in my early twenties with concomitant vision loss. At first, the loss of peripheral vision manifests as night blindness and difficulty seeing in panorama. Then the visual fields constrict until one day, someday, too-soon-day, today there is little left, then none. Now I have only one "working" eye and one degree of vision, and no depth perception or binocular vision. Everything I see is blurred, as if through an opaque, green-pea-soup lens. I run into doorways, which shift. I'm uncertain as to the properties and placement of things. Faces are gone, so I can't tell who people are. This can be amusing, awkward, or embarrassing. And since I can't locate little children, I'm in a hypervigilant state until a small voice shouts, "Over *here*, Mummy," but *here* isn't the name or direction of a place. And always, in the foreground, the landscape shifts under my feet, because what I see doesn't always intersect with reality. Misconstructions abound. Sometimes I feel like a seaworn glass bottle that was shattered and then worn smooth in remnants by the wash of the surf. I'm scattered—one piece on the shore here, another miles away, still others in the deeps. I can only sense or imagine the original from the fragments. The whole is gone forever.

There's beauty in these fragments of china, stone, and glass—a sea change that transforms them into objects rich and beautiful. But I don't feel this yet. I only see the loss of the once-known and still-wanted.

* * *

I have lived all my life by the coast. While I'm not a surfer or sunbaker, the sand, sea, scrub, and surf contour the geography I occupy. It's my foreshore—the Harbour, Woolloomooloo, Garden Island, Rushcutters Bay, Darling Point, Edgecliff, Double Bay, and Point Piper. Here, we find secret beaches, millionaires' homes, and yachting clubs, all under the Southern Cross. Some boast only glimpses, others have views of Sydney Harbour in full sail and bloom.

These coastal landmarks are within a walk or short bus ride from my home. At the center of my universe, even as my senses fade, is the city's harbor—not just a beautiful body of history and water, but a working harbor. If you stay in a hotel on its edge, I'm told, you can be lulled to sleep by gentle horns and the chugs of boats, water taxis, ferries, and grand ocean liners devouring and disgorging passengers. I can no longer see the Opera House on Bennelong Point, but I know she's there. When I was a girl, we made a special family excursion shortly after its completion, to gaze in wonder at her sails.

Thousands of years ago, this land was a tidal island inhabited by the Gadigal First People, who fished, laughed, sang, danced, held corroborees, and told stories here. Our postcolonial legacy is far reaching, damaging, and damning (our country is long overdue for a reckoning and recognition of our First Peoples' sovereignty). There is something sweet in this bitter legacy about the land being a continuous storytelling domain. A few of the littoral landmarks have reclaimed their names: the Opera House rightly sits not on Bennelong Point but on Gadigal land known as Tubowgule, or "the meeting of waters." The harbor is a Gadigal place.

John Olsen, one of Australia's great artists, died in 2023 at ninety-five. Before the Opera House mural, Olsen completed a smaller painting called "Five Bells" (1963), held by the Art Gallery of New South Wales. We have a print in our sitting room, a testament to how locals are wedded to Sydney Harbour. We may flirt with other coastal regions—have affairs with the warm waters of Balinese, Greek, Italian, or Hawaiian beaches—but we hanker, always, for our harbor's variable blue-green-gray depths, with its shifting coastline contours and urban encroachments.

* * *

My sensory impairments impinge on my competencies: I'm not freestyling but dog-paddling on my residuals. Sometimes, often, I'm beached on the shores of not knowing what is going on, for neither sense is able to help the other out. Vision is down to that lone degree of distorted central vision. Hearing loss is profound, not good at all for sense-making even with supercharged hearing aids. I grab at single words as drowning folk grasp at rescue, and attempt to wrestle some sense of topic, conversational direction, or import. Too often, I'm wrong. "Full moon in Paris" becomes "four million parrots." Funny but dangerous, too—as when "three" sounds like "thirteen" sounds like "thirty" units of insulin or milligrams of medication. I mistake the car and get into a stranger's vehicle (he was understanding and helped me return to my family). At an art gallery, I put my arm around my husband—not my husband. I don't see the rock pool at my favorite beach and land heavily, brokenly. People, places, and things are all mired in uncertainty.

Anxiety and uncertainty escalate as such things occur. R. D. Laing's concept of "ontological insecurity" captures my erosive situation. Laing defines ontological security as the desired state of trust, reliability, and predictability in information, which promotes a sense of knowing what is going on. As Laing wrote in his 1965 book *The Divided Self*: "a man may have a sense of his presence in the world as a real, alive, whole, and, in a temporal sense, a continuous person. As such, he can live out into the world and meet others: a world and others experienced as equally real, alive, whole, and continuous." In this state of confidence, according to Laing, a person can manage the "hazards of life" (1965, 39).

From where I write—from deafblindness—land, liminal coast, and sea have become hazardous. The consequences of an ontologically insecure state are, to quote Laing again, "greater anxieties and dangers" (67). Confidence in encountered environments (as well as in people and things) is essential for security, trust, and identity. Anthony Giddens, writing almost thirty years after Laing, discusses in *Modernity and Self-Identity* how anxiety is generated in situations characterized by failures of ontological security—from free-floating general anxiety to anxieties "pinned to items, traits or situations" (1991, 44). I embody such theorizing. The prospect of boarding a ferry, bus, or train provokes angst; the thought of a beach stroll, bush walk, or visit to my local shops up the hill provokes emotional distress. It's more than not seeing and not hearing. It's that land and water prove unreliable. The land lies.

I reconciled to hearing loss early, but not seeing "does my head in," as the colloquialism goes. Impaired senses mean that the environment (even when familiar) is deceptive, and this enflames psychological distress. Reduced information creates uncertainty which, in turn, affects self-confidence, because those of us with impaired or absent sight and hearing cannot rely on what is seen and heard. And it's not just when we're out and about that we are vulnerable to unpredictable environments. In our homes, too, tricks of light, sleight of unseen objects on the floor, an unexpectedly open cupboard door, a toppled chair—all can cause injury. So too does social life become fraught, as our ability to read people and situations disappears. It becomes hard to maintain connection, with social worlds shrinking as the physical recedes.

But there's more. Compounding these difficulties (which sometimes feel insurmountable) is having to negotiate the hostility of human-created and perpetuated barriers, both physical and attitudinal. Ableist microaggressions are rife. Have you ever tried to get an accessible form from a hospital, bank, realtor, funding body, or city council office? Heard "Are you deaf or something?" in a queue or "You don't *look* disabled" on a bus? Been labeled as drunk or drug-affected because you're wobbly on your feet? Such experiences complicate our lives along with the burdens of everyday existence. We get heartbroken, too. Our parents need care. We have children, and we wish we had jobs, or better bosses, or higher pay. And the constant changes and adjustments of degenerative sensory loss impose additional ontological-security burdens. Periods of adjustment to new sensory encroachments may be prolonged; sometimes further worsening occurs before we've gotten used to the previous one.

Those lines of Slessor's poem about the drowning of Joe Lynch come to mind in the wake of exponential sensory losses. Slessor writes that *something* remains even when the significance of Joe Lynch's name has dissolved—but that something is a remnant that rails against its circumstances: "And hits and cries against the ports of space, / Beating their sides to make its fury heard." I'd like the fury of losing communication senses to remain articulate and persuasive, even when confronted with isolating, desolating loss. And I worry, too, that protections and policies aren't enough to ensure that every person, every institution, will practice inclusion. I worry that not everyone walks the accessibility talk, which jeopardizes socially just supports for all of us with disabilities.

* * *

Sensory erosion: uncertainty of information, communication failures, unsteady terrain. It's a complex bio-psycho-emotional process, and it's environmentally challenging. All space turns liminal; solid ground becomes soft sand. Walk on soft sand and there's the thrill of the tide swirling around your feet, waves hitting your ankles and then your knees. But then the dread of a possible fall down mossy stairs into a rock pool, off a jetty or a boat, of a simple misstep from a sandbar into deep water. Turn too quickly and there's no visible geo-marker to locate the safety of the shore. My facility for reading coastlines and problem solving has been affected by reduced stimuli, along with my increased communication and mobility needs. And so my resources for navigating life's hazards diminish. Often, I am not at home in my own territory. I am in what could be termed *displacia*.

I live with the enormity of nostalgia for shorelines that are no longer in my sightlines. ("Nostalgia" combines the Greek *nosta*, "home," and *algia*, "pain.") Algesia grips as the way-markers of my coastlines fade. When I can't orientate myself in my street, let alone in my harbor, I lose remembered detail. The Harbour Bridge, in my sight, is no longer a feat of engineering, the Sydney Opera House no longer the visually commanding Queen of Circular Quay. Lost, too, are so many treasured faces, places, and things. Sometimes I wonder: if I can't see them, do they still exist? Am I unmoored entirely from my home shores? (But of course, they exist with corporeal solidity if I bump, tap, stumble, or fall onto them.) Disconnected from geography and terrain, I am tethered to others for almost all acts of daily living. No more solo ferry therapy; instead, I wait for a sighted-hearing companion to buy the ticket, help me board the boat, warn of trip hazards, walk the beaches by my side, pick up sea glass and marvel with me at its smooth edges. I am told of the green-blue opaqueness.

Though I fight the fact that people with deafblindness are dependent on others, I also accept that reality. In the acceptance comes a surprising return and reconnection to geography, as sighted guides shepherd me to lost places. I don't find *exactly* what was lost. Communication guides can describe the environment, but they have ideas about what information they think I want, and I'm ambivalent about being told what I can't view for myself. *Replacia* is someplace new and mutable. We're all learning this new shoreline together, my team and I, through tactile fingerspelling, speech to texting, tactile sign, and (with tentative steps) sign language. I feel the Australian sign for "beach/seaside/waves" as I move my hands over my companion's. Both arms sway away from the body like water undulating to salute the shore.

Everything takes longer, as relaying information and detail lengthens every activity. To borrow Slessor's words, I am less bound by "Time that is moved by little fidget wheels"—it is "not my time." And in this elongation of time, there is mindfulness—in the act of touching places, people, things. Paradoxically, I find art again, especially the impasto technique of palette knife creations. After a helper's descriptions, I buy my first piece. The young impasto oil painter, Emily Persson, delivers a tactile, petaled experience in the foreground, with robust, raised leaves framing an off-center smoothness, in her trademark keyhole vista. And within the aperture of the painting is the sea, the work suggesting possibilities to come. I'm heartened by the fact that there is figurative light in this physical darkness, that adversity can bring more than gloom and doom.

From too long a time in *displacia*—where the seashore is a hostile, deceptive force—to the present moment, the land lies differently. There is a sort of re-placement. The land *feels* now.

* * *

Just before COVID-19, I spend a month at Pearl Beach. At first, I resist all attempts at a beach or bush walk. No, no—happy to stay inside, touching predictable furniture in a familiar space. Then, one overcast day, when the kookaburra has left his perch and a lone bush turkey follows, I venture out, along with my companion. On the shore's edge, I relive the visceral thrill of water eddying and flowing around my feet, smell the brine, and later taste salt on hot chips. I am almost undone by the pleasure of it all.

I experience life through a keyhole—with fragmented words and my one degree of murky central vision hinting at what lies beyond. My sighted companion fills in the detail. As we clamber over the rocks to the tidal pool at Pearl Beach, it becomes manifest. The ground is *predictably* unpredictable. And the tactile messaging from my companion—my human support—is responsive and expansive. My world is no longer narrow. I rediscover what has been lost as something new. This is not a restoration or restitution tale: it is adjustment, a summoning of taste, smell, and touch as conduits to meaning. And joy, peace even.

Still, I feel a constant, barely submerged mourning for the lost colors and contours of sightlines. I have notions of green, but they're slipping. The language of color now supersedes my visual experience as it's superimposed on my memories of green, a beloved shade. Is it emerald? Mint? Jade or olive? Viridian, perhaps. Or bottle green. Maybe it is sea green. Green in memory is multichromatic. I especially miss shades of green near coastal water in New South Wales. All the different tones of eucalyptus, from olive to khaki, and the silvery green-gray of salt scrub. I ache for all the variants of green that aren't murky pea soup.

As I walk on a shore with a guide who can re-describe (and so, re-inscribe) the sandy green and blue landscape, as we traverse, touch, feel and taste it, I re-place myself in a braver, newer, differently complex world.

* * *

People living with deafblindness display a vast heterogeneity. They speak a multitude of languages (including variants of haptic and sign), experience widely variable residual senses, and have disparate access to and ownership of assistive technologies. These facts mean that without social recognition and proper consultation, without planning and preparedness, they—we—are vulnerable in disasters. The pandemic was a time of unmaking.

Although everyone lost geography, space, and mobility during the crisis, shelter-in-place policies and lockdowns particularly restricted support and safety for the deafblind and infirm. In such situations, people with deafblindness become exiles, along with many older citizens. If you don't have devices, don't have internet access, don't have training, don't have senses to navigate, don't have dexterity, don't have support, then the global move online may have kept you offline. Online learning, online shopping, online entertainments, and telehealth—while these have become the norm, they are neither universally accessible nor deafblind friendly. We become forcibly displaced persons, the banished, even in our own cities.

As I was reclaiming the world (with assistance), the virus dis-located me from proxy embodiment; as shelter-in-place practices became the norm, I was removed from newfound geography—my renewed love of coast effectively beached. Then, when the first restrictions were lifted, our state government suggested and sanctioned picnicking for the vaccinated. A picnic would be an opportunity to recover my land. We found a spot down from Observatory Hill overlooking Sydney Harbour. We ate chicken sandwiches on thick slices of bread and drank fizzy mineral water. We sat close to the pylons and in the shadow of the Harbour Bridge. We had a direct line of sight to the Opera House (even though it's the faintest of blurs to me). There were no tourists—an extraordinary thing, as our chosen site is normally busy with foot traffic and newlyweds having photos taken with the Harbour and Opera House as backdrops. We finished our meal with chocolate-coated strawberries. We had a thermos of hot water and quality tea bags. We lay down on our rug, propped up on our elbows. There were fewer ferries, not so many passing cars, and no passenger liners. The sun shone, and I experienced the waters, vicariously, as sapphire blue. It felt like reclamation.

Fast forward to October, Freedom Day, when most Sydney inhabitants were double-vaccinated. There were caveats for those most at risk—that they should stay at home, still take care. Liberty was not for everybody; our community was encouraged to exercise "personal responsibility" and "common sense," to stay in self-imposed lockdown if being outside was dangerous. This effectively meant that "society" was only for the fit, able, and young. But COVID-19 seems less of a disaster these days, more of a nuisance. I write now from a place less apart, less homebound. As the roars of the pandemic diminish, I can hold my city's harbor and her glorious coastlines in my mind's eye, at my fingertips and feet, on my taste buds—and always with the scent of salt on the wind.

Works Cited

Giddens, Anthony. 1991. *Modernity and Self-Identity: Self and Society in the Late Modern Age.* Cambridge: Polity Press.

Laing, R. D. 1965. *The Divided Self: An Existential Study in Sanity and Madness.* Harmondsworth, Middlesex: Penguin Books.

Slessor, Kenneth. 1939. *Five Bells: XX Poems.* Sydney: Frank C. Johnson.

16

Body Workers

Ellen Samuels

Madison, WI, 2007

As soon as I arrived in Wisconsin, I scheduled a massage at my new gym, tucking a two-page article about Ehlers-Danlos syndrome into my purse. I wanted the therapist to know that if she pulled—however lightly—on my arms or legs, I would stretch till I snapped like an old rubber band. She was young, blond, wore blue eyeliner on her blue eyes.

I lay face down under the sheet, waiting to feel her hands on me. Just as her touch whispered across my back, I heard her gentle voice in my ear.

"Ellen, I believe in God and I believe in a god that heals. Would it be okay if I pray for you now?" I was entirely naked except for my small cotton briefs.

"Please don't," is what I answered. I don't remember the rest.

Ithaca, NY, 1996

When I finally needed a disabled parking pass, I was twenty-four years old, in graduate school for creative writing. It seemed as if moving to New York had made my body start breaking apart, injuries spreading like the indigo-ice fractures of Finger Lake springtime.

E. Samuels (✉)
Departments of English and Gender & Women's Studies,
University of Wisconsin-Madison, Madison, WI, USA
e-mail: ejsamuels@wisc.edu

In my first year, my hands had gnarled with mysterious pain till I couldn't even write my name. I spent months at the occupational-therapy table at Tompkins County Hospital, arms plunged deep in machines whirling corn husks and hot air, wrists sticky with ultrasound gel, thumbs locked into lint-ugly splints. After ten months of treatment, I was finally able again to grip a fork or pen.

But just a few weeks later, when I reached for a book overhead, an acid wire sang the length of my right leg from heel to coccyx, making every step a stutter and gasp. Invisible inside, my sciatic nerve had turned in on itself, was trapped like a hand in a slammed door.

Health insurance paid for twice-weekly visits to a kindly chiropractor whose elbow drilled into my hip joints, slowly unthreading nerve from bone, and counting to ten as I breathed through the backroads of pain.

Two months into treatment, she sat back and sighed. "Usually with this injury your muscles would be short and tight. But yours, yours are long and weak. That's why it's taking so long to heal."

She sent me to swim every day in the YMCA's frigid pool, my teeth chattering through every slow, long lap. Gradually, over months, the pain eased. I could walk again.

She made me better. I trusted her completely.

Cambridge, MA, 1998

Barbara, my poetry teacher, said that the massage therapists at the Shiatsu Institute lifted her skull right up and out of her worries. My left shoulder blade had been clamoring its trouble, keeping me awake for weeks. I lay on a cloth mat while a thin white woman shoved her thumbs up and down my spine.

At the end of the hour, she asked how I felt. I told her the truth. My shoulder still hurt.

"Do you drink water?" she asked. "Green tea, miso soup?"

I nodded uncertainly.

"Then you know what the problem is," she said quietly, her green-gray eyes fixed on mine. "It's you. You must want this. You are making this happen."

I paid and left, her words knocking together in my belly—limestone, granite, sediment of the Eastern seaboard.

Madison, WI, 2008

My walking never really recovered. By age thirty-five, I could barely make it through the grocery store, gripping the cart's edge till my hands knew its shape all day. My new colleagues kept telling me how many miles of bike trail Madison had, how smooth the lanes for skiing in winter. I drove from home to office to grocery store, windows rolled up tight.

I asked my new physical therapist if it was perhaps time for a wheelchair.

"Oh no," she answered quickly. "No. I don't recommend that at all." She pushed her sandy hair back with one hand and frowned. "It would be, it's just, emotionally crippling."

"But how am I supposed to get around?" I was embarrassed by how my voice broke. I had waited three months for this appointment.

"Not like that." Her forehead an autumn-furrowed field. "Not like that."

Middletown, CA, 2003

The road to Harbin Hot Springs was steep and winding, a narrow snake of rust-colored dirt. We crept warily downward in my old Civic, my foot worrying the brake pedal.

I hadn't seen a naked man since college. My wife laughed gently, told me to relax, floated like an otter in the communal pool while I spent my birthday money on a long massage. The bodyworker was tanned, bearded, hair pulled into a scraggly knot. I was relieved he wore a crimson sarong knotted around his lean hips.

He set a brass bowl on my belly to collect toxins as he released them inside me, lying flat in his clearing of weeping trees, asking how long I'd had pain, how I lived with it.

"It sounds like you've tried everything to get better," he said, as he dug into the taut muscle of my neck. "Eating well, acupuncture, massage."

His thumb traced a gully along my first rib. "You know what we say, then? *It's the issue behind the tissue.* It's something you're holding onto that you need to let go."

"No." My voice seemed loud under the electric-blue sky. I turned my whole head to look at him, his surprised face. "No," I kept saying.

West Lafayette, IN, 1972–1984

The bodyworker I saw as a child in Indiana was not a worker or a body. I was not a body then, only a collection of parts.

A doctor told my mother my hips had dislocated while I was still inside her. There was nothing to be done.

My knees would always turn toward each other instead of facing ahead. My body was always talking to itself, and listening.

17

Never in One Place: On Waking in a Different Body

Anand Prahlad

> I went down to the crossroads...
> —Robert Johnson

I live in my body, mind, and spirit in a five-bedroom house, in a quiet and friendly suburb in the small college town of Columbia, Missouri, halfway between St. Louis and Kansas City. In the Midwest, United States. In North America in the Western Hemisphere, at 38.951561 latitude and 92.328636 longitude. On Earth (the third planet from the sun in the known solar system), in the Milky Way galaxy. In "our" universe, in the multiverse. I have lived in this body for sixty-seven years, in this city for thirty-one years, and in this house for twelve. I live here the way an astronaut lives in a space capsule. Or the way a clownfish lives in a coral reef. Because any place is inside of another place, and that place is inside of another place, and so on and so on, like Russian nesting dolls, like the universe. And every place is inside a space, that is inside some other space, and on and on with spaces.

My body is inside so many places, all day long, sometimes one at a time, sometimes all at once. Like Gregor in Franz Kafka's *Metamorphosis,* this other unrecognizable body has slowly grown in place of the one that I knew, the one I loved, and that had been my steady companion. The one I was married to before I was married to anyone else. I am still me—or at least I think I

A. Prahlad (✉)
University of Missouri, Columbia, MO, USA
e-mail: Prahlada@missouri.edu

am—but my body doesn't listen to the rest of me the way it used to. It doesn't go when and where my mind goes. It doesn't quiver or exhale with the joy of my spirit. It's no longer "mine" in the same way it once was, and I suppose "I" am no longer it. We walk together, side-by-side, half inside of each other, like an object and a shadow, not sure which of us is which. We eat separate meals at the same meal time, lie down together but have separate sleep and dreams. We watch the world through separate eyes, and inside separate minds whirl separate imaginations. And my body is never quite the same today as it was yesterday. As if it's not even solid, but a liquid thing, sometimes fire, sometimes water, sometimes ice or steam, and sometimes air or earth. To most others, it looks pretty much the same. Or it could be that they don't know quite what to say about the difference—or if they should say anything.

It can't run, this new body. It can't swim. It can hardly walk a city block. It can't get from one airline gate to another without a wheelchair and assistance. It can't jump or garden or do yard work or cut and saw wood and make things. It can't lift or exercise. It can play musical instruments, for a little while, but it can't entirely enjoy the experience. If I used to have one hundred gallons of energy in a day, on my best days now I have maybe twenty. And if I ever cheat, and go over my daily quota, by even a little, I pay for it dearly in the weeks to come. This new body has little appetite. Few tastes. It knows limited realms of pleasure, and the ones it knows are muted. And because my memory hardly ever worked anyway, in the best of times, I can't remember what a lot of pleasures were really like.

My body—a ship leaving port and crossing the sea with other chained bodies—may have arrived some time ago, resting comfortably in the harbor. But the slower shadow of the ship has now finally arrived. And today is inside six previous decades, and all the places and spaces my body had been in, as though today's stories didn't begin today but exist inside all the other stories of my life. And I'm not as certain as Eli Clare when he writes, "The body as home but only if it is understood that the stolen body can be reclaimed" (2015, 13). Can it always be, at least in the material realm, beyond ideology?

And the thing about my body and its illnesses is that sickness strips me of the clothes I need to pass for normal in the world. It strips my mind of how to dress myself. I'm left standing there naked, hands too busy to cover up. Sickness takes all of my attention, as if I am so engrossed in a film that when someone yells "Fire," I don't hear them. Or as if I'm concentrating on juggling bowling pins, and someone asks me to count backward from one hundred in multiples of three. Sickness hands me a long list of "I-can-no-longer-do-thats." Like: seem to understand, even when I don't. Like: pretend to hear words that actually come across as background sounds of traffic, birds, clothes

17 Never in One Place: On Waking in a Different Body

rustling. Like: think as clearly. Interpret. Translate twenty words, ten gestures, ten facial expressions, and ten postures simultaneously. Like: speak, communicate. Understand feelings. Like: not laugh at things out of the blue. Not melt down.

This new body can't go for hikes on trails through the parks—either roughened dirt ones that wind through forest trees and undergrowth, or those with even, asphalted lanes for bikes. It can't walk around mirrored lakes as geese make expanding V-ripples in the water. Instead, I take to carpeted paths from the bedroom to the study, or hearth room, bathroom, or kitchen. Working on my balance. Stretching my thighs and calves as best I can. Listening to my breath. Noticing the birds or rabbits out the windows, taking over the yard. Reflecting on the growth of young trees, planted a few years ago. A dansom plum gifted by a friend. A fast-growing willow. A spruce sapling that was dying, but is now vibrant with tender, green shoots. A crabapple that had no leaves for its first few years, because Japanese beetles devoured them. The head-sized white blossoms of hydrangeas out front. The purple sage and hollyhocks.

* * *

Aut/Chemo/Fibro
water touching/the skin/and burning/a hot iron/branding flesh/showers/of cigar tips/razor edges/sustained/operatic notes/of pain/in muscles/missing from/Michelangelo's/sketches/of the body/or med school/diagrams/and into/that invisible/tissue, that/supposedly/non-existent/phantom/flesh/erratic/bayonets/lunging/and then/turning.

* * *

Tonight it will rain and the basement will flood, the way it has most days for the last few months. All earth here, you see, is clay, and little drains as it should. If you have a basement, the local wisdom goes, you have a heap of trouble. And so, the house you covet and one day can move into becomes a kind of purgatory. Each morning when I wake up falling back to earth, my eyes slowly opening as the air rushes by and the sky seems to be funneling. And then I crash down, fully awake, and something like laughter runs through my body. Because even falling, I have nothing like fear. The trees have agreed never to impale me with their limbs, and the earth has agreed never to break my bones. But I'm counting the times the floor creaks. Or the pipes pitch tantrums, or groan. The refrigerator clicks or buzzes or whines like a kitten. Metal in the furnace clicks against other metal. A phantom squirrel scurries in the air vent. A popping in the wall like when a nursing baby lets go of a nipple. A crack around a window frame. A tilt in the floor of the kitchen I can't remember being there the day before. And for a while, I stand there, watching from different directions and angles, trying to tell if I'm only imagining the unevenness.

I put my mask on and drag my body down the stairs, plug in the cord for the power vac, flip the switch and begin vacuuming up water. Even when a day passes without rain, the ground is so soaked through that the small trickles and waterfalls gushing through cracks in the foundation keep coming. And by now, everything is damp, moldy. When did this all begin, I ask myself? How did things come to this?

And then I'm back living in a shack my body once stayed in, in the Blue Mountains in Jamaica. All alone with spirits of Maroons and Sister Nanny and the thick foliage of akee, tamarind, pimento. Cassia, lignum vitae (or "ligany," as some Jamaicans call it). Frangipani, jacaranda, and palm. Lying on a cot, in the heat, while a soft breeze blows through paneless windows, along with voices of barking dogs, reggae, and someone calling out from a distant yard. Feeling some ancient, indescribable blackness. Vibe. Spirit. Feeling some ancient earth. My body is young again and every muscle is as taut as the cables of the Brooklyn and melodic as those of the Sutong Yangtze River Bridge. Every heartbeat is a song from the earth's beginning, and every breath a celebration, the first buds on a flower stalk with dreams of opening. In full innocence, I leave my one-room, doorless "Inn," all my belongings in a suitcase and bag on the funky cot, and make my way down the hill for the day's adventure. The sun sinks deeply into me, ebbing like waters through the dark windows of my skin, and I am outside of time.

* * *

The drone of the power vac reminds me of oak. The immense ancient tree that once stood beside our house, its giant limbs defying any disbelief one could have about the grandeur, power, or surreality of nature. Is that when it began? When a branch fell, striking the porch, and covering the entire spacious back yard. It was only then that we appreciated its true immensity, which we never would have fathomed simply gazing up, or even looking from a nearby distance. Stepping among the branches of its fallen limb was like walking through a whale carcass washed up on a beach. Its size memorialized me, and I was lost in the colors it evoked. The tastes on my tongue when I touched the bark of its branches—and especially when I held on to the crooks where smaller

17 Never in One Place: On Waking in a Different Body

branches grew out of larger ones—overwhelmed all of my senses. It was more than my mind could quite grasp, no matter how many times I returned to it. And because the oak had a sickness that couldn't be cured, its interior being slowly eaten away; and because it was likely that other limbs would eventually break and fall; and because to leave it standing meant risking property and even lives, we had to have it taken down. Was that when this began? This period of trials, of darkness? Did my body live in that tree, and the tree live in my body? I wonder sometimes, because shortly after the oak collapsed, I was diagnosed with cancer.

* * *

Now I'm back in my childhood home, in rural Virginia, on a screened-in porch with my mother, and my father, listening to them talk. On a summer evening lit only by the light of a half moon and stars, lost and found, enveloped in the thick forest sounds of crickets, frogs, and cicadas. They've put a blanket around me, even though its warm, because my body keeps shaking with a fever. I leave them, becoming cicada, and my tears on the papery surface of my wings deepen my singing. From my height in a large maple, I can see the blurred lights of fireflies, twinkling on and off, and before I know it, I'm singing to patterns of light I once thought were random. And into the patterns of light, all of us are singing. The cicadas and frogs and crickets and whippoorwills and owls. And into each other's patterns we go, taste and dissolve and flow, turning curves in a road, ascending and descending, riding currents of air and warmth, gradually building to a burst every three minutes like stars quietly exploding.

In one burst, I'm thrown out of the loop, like a dazed parachutist hitting ground. I'm in the kitchen of the plantation Big House, with my Great-Great-Great-Cousin Lucy. She is boiling water in a big iron pot on a wood-burning stove, and peeling white potatoes. Lucy doesn't speak much, or even hum, and only a few others can understand her. She taps on things or makes sounds, her private Morse codes. When she sees me, she taps her knife to say *I'm glad you've come*, and we go on in the calm space of no speech, in the house that is momentarily emptied of other bodies. While outside, someone is chopping wood, the sound of logs splitting raising hair on my arms. And someone is brushing a horse, and the horse whinnies. And someone is hoeing in a garden. And someone is plucking feathers from a slaughtered chicken. And someone is feeding hay to the cows, and a cow is mooing. I love my Cousin Lucy. And love, too, is a place, a space, unconfined, without boundaries, they say. She doesn't know, but I do, that two years from now, after the slave owner has gotten tired of her and moved on to some other soft black body . . . after his wife finally sees her chance. I know because I read it in the archives, a century later, in a letter she wrote to her brother. They'll have her taken to the Central Lunatic Asylum, in Petersburg, and have her committed as a "person of unsound mind."

The drone of the power vac reminds me of oak. Of the C note of the chainsaw when they were cutting the fallen limb into smaller pieces. More men, making more noises, will be coming soon to install the drainage system and anchors in the foundation walls to keep the house from collapsing. I shudder to think of the sound of the jackhammer in the basement. On good days, I could drive the short distance to the park, and if the weather permitted, walk a little way around the lake and find a bench and sit for hours, reading, or just watching the language of lake ripples and geese drifting toward and away from the banks. The sounds of children in the playground. Cardinals and sparrows. The soft waves of wind exposing the undersides of leaves and reshaping the curves of my skin. But what will I do if the men show up on one of my bad days, when I can't remember things or when my body can barely move? If I have to greet them and let them in, and then lie in bed as the house shakes, along with my bed and my body, as if everything is about to explode? And what if that day, on my ladder of thought levels, I can only manage rungs one, two, and three?

* * *

My different levels of thought:
Level one—where am I?
Level two—what's happening with my body?
Level three—who am I?
Level four—where am I supposed to be?
Level five—where am I in time?
Level six—what is the proper distance from other objects (and bodies)?
Level seven—what language should I be speaking?
Level eight—what and where are the exits?
Level nine—what is the danger level?
Level ten—what instruments are playing in the orchestra of my senses?
Level eleven—what notes are they playing?
Level twelve—when is when?
Level thirteen—are we adding, subtracting, multiplying, or dividing?
Level fourteen—what shapes are in the equation?
Level fifteen—what are the solids and what are the liquids?

* * *

17 Never in One Place: On Waking in a Different Body

Our house, our house, our house, our house, our house! Our house in a deciduous forest, in a small clearing, in Columbia, in the Midwest, in the U.S., in the national state of unrest, in the raging time of the COVID pandemic, in the early years of climate-change disaster, in the twenty-first century, on planet Earth. Not every autist is as bound by routine as I am, as likely to lose breath, or reason, or ability to know, and do, and remember, or to lose their sense of safety if a routine drops like a glass pitcher and breaks into many pieces. Not every autist is going constantly in and out of blue, or pink, or chameleon, or princess. Not every autist is so obsessed with the smallest details of their rooms or of the world outdoors, or weeps if temperatures, sounds, or light fluctuate fractions of degrees, or if objects are moved inches. Not every autist would necessarily feel the weight and ache of a house as if it was their own body. Or when push comes to shove would rather be inside, in square rooms, where corners are ever-present points of rescue, solace, or sanctuary. And where, when necessary, outside can never enter, except certain sounds and light—or a breeze that lives in cells and resonances beyond any time, upon and beneath their skin. But one cannot help being who they are.

As with my body, as with our house, the planet is changing. The air is no longer the same. The quality of shadows. The textures of light. The angles of things. The colors of leaves and blossoms, and the taste of the wind. The seasons. The buds of bulbs and branches. Bird calls. Rain showers. Wind. Temperatures are off. Sometimes because the wind has been strangled in a far-off country. Or because some waves have been overheated in the Atlantic or chilled too much in the Arctic or the Baltic. Or sea currents are grieving in the Pacific. Or butterflies are dying on an island, and so the wind from their wings never reaches the mainland. Or canaries have found only desolate land at the end of their migration and their songs are never sung. Hence, the vibrations from their throats never become airborne, and the leaves in parts of the world, like Missouri, are never touched with those vibrations. Those that give the shade of trees their sweetness, the wind from leaves their textures of solace.

The forest animals are no longer sure where the borders are and have begun more and more crossings. Ants stream across the kitchen counters and up into the cabinets. No matter how small, an ant sensing my presence can paralyze me. So it is with ants, and water, and sometimes wasps and fruit flies, spiders, chiggers, ticks, mosquitos, and even a mouse fleeing into my space as if escaping a forest fire—as if my body, my place, is an ark that's going to save them. Poison ivy that once grew in small pockets out near the shed now claims space in the borders around the house, teeth latching onto brick and climbing as tall as trees. Scientists say that increased levels of CO_2 have led to poison ivy "on steroids." The rabbits populating the yard. A red fox that runs by sometimes in the early morning fog frightening me. The deer eating buds from my hibiscus now inclined to simply stare me down. One of the large hawks that nests in a neighbor's tall tree, and often comes and sits on our fence, listening patiently. Even bear spottings in towns not far away.

But the animals are also coming closer because I have been so absent from the yard. I used to always be tending things. Planting and pruning. Digging and clipping. Moving stone and wood and making things. Making designs. Shapes. Patterns. Making beauty. Sidewalks and patios of pavers, borders of bricks and stones. Flower beds and compost bins. Sheds, arbors, and fences. Powerwashing sidewalks and siding. Sawing, sanding, and hammering. Measuring, mitering, and painting.

If you buy a house in a suburb of nice houses, and your house is not quite as nice as many others. And if you are black and you are your only black neighbor. You might consider hiring someone to do some landscaping, painting, and all the other things that would make your house nicer. Because even if you're like me, in a neighborhood like mine, where most of the neighbors are white professionals. Doctors, professors, health-care workers, teachers, real-estate agents, artists. Where you can own a five-bedroom house for a fraction of what it would cost in places on the coasts. Where there are Black Lives Matter signs in a number of the front yards. Where most of your neighbors are friendly, there will still be those who aren't friendly at all.

There are always those things, you know. The mailbox broken down. The lawn jockey. The calls to the city about a single weed in your yard. The aggressions toward your kids. The eyes out the window as you pass. Comfortable, yes, but not entirely at home. Sometimes like oil and water. Like fire and paper. Like a gazelle on an African veldt, where lions also live. Like a deer in the woods, anywhere near humans. Like a tree in most forests of the world. You would like your house to look nicer, just for yourself and your family, but there's always that wave of pressure, that rush of panic in your belly. That flush of embarrassment blowing like wind against your cheeks. That feeling of nakedness, like being on the toilet in a dream without walls, in public. That feeling of being like Mr. Biswas, in V. S. Naipaul's classic novel, fighting against all odds.

Coming to live in a house and the houses we come to live in, like our bodies, and where they come to at any point in time, are only parts of a larger story—only one place and space inside of others. Like wealth is a place, a space. Like poverty, being poor. Like being white, or black, or Asian, or Native American. Like being "healthy," or ill, and all the different kinds of illnesses are their own places. Like having a job, and where your job is, and who your job is with, or not having a job. All spaces. Like being "disabled" in different countries, times, cities, towns, or communities. Like being in a family. Like gardening, listening to, or playing music, reading a book, watching television, dancing. Like sleeping, or dreaming. Like being out of your body, or outside your mind. Like remembering or not remembering or forgetting are places and spaces of their own. As Lennard J. Davis notes, "there is no division between the world of the body and world of the body politic" (111).

All things considered, though, I really like where I live. Yes, like almost all American towns and cities, ours is a testimony to the spirit of determination. But also, like in other places, there is a certain sadness in our beauty, a certain tragedy in our grace. If only, instead of saying we live in a city, we could say first that we live in a forest, in a cleared-out stretch of land we temporarily occupy. That would change so many things. Like slipping into another body. Or if we could say, in a desert. Or on a mountain. Or in a floodplain or prairie. And that the forest was here first, and will be here when we're gone, and is always trying to restore itself, to rid itself of us. That the forest determines us, no matter how many towers we build. We fight it, those of us here in my neighborhood, and in neighborhoods like mine across the country. We have been fighting it for centuries with every ounce of our being.

Even at that, I confess that at times I relish the comfort of our delusions, the material comforts they bring. I share the imagined safety. The beauty of such manicured sharp angles, all rectangles and squares of flattened green grasses, reddened and painted brick, sand-colored steps and concrete chapters, slopes of white and gray asphalt roof shingles, all intertwined and suspended in time like the geometries of an Escher painting. It's not perfect, but I can have many perfect moments here.

For someone like me, who is middle class, black and disabled, it's not a bad place to be. It's easy to get around. The traffic is generally slow. It's liberal. I can get healthy food. Medical people are really attentive, almost like the old-fashioned doctors in small towns one hundred years ago. It's full of trees. Lots of old growth and greenery everywhere most of the year. Everyone in my neighborhood has trees in their yards, and all of the streets are lined with trees. Everywhere in the city, there are trees. In the daytime, the trees bring the sky and clouds closer, while at the same time keeping them far away. At night, their silhouettes are like arms around me, so many shades of black and gray against the lightness of what we thought was a blackened sky. So many shades against the distant brightness of moon and stars, shades of black that turn black into its own spectrum, like those in a Kerry James Marshall painting.

And then, there's streetlights on my street, making it magical, no matter what the weather—fog or mist or pure and silent stillness.

In the morning, an occasional car goes by. Young children on bikes sowing their voices in the midday light. A small dog barking from behind a fence as a woman walks by with her dog on a leash. A scent of emptiness I can't decipher. Certainly, it has something to do with life, the natural world, and our bodies rubbing against the American Dream. With the awkward place that my black and disabled mind and body holds in American stories. With the way that even in this lovely setting, I hesitate to go out for a walk. For if, as Rosemarie Garland-Thompson notes, "physical instability is the bodily manifestation of political anarchy" (1997, 43), then I must be the ultimate anarchist. Some of my impulse to hide is pride, yes. Not wanting neighbors to see my feebleness. It's not that they're unkind, quite the contrary. People out walking will sometimes stop to talk if I'm gathering the mail. A few will ask how I'm doing, and really mean it. But I don't want their pity. As David T. Mitchell and Sharon L. Snyder write in describing narrative prosthesis, "the deficient body, by virtue of its insufficiency, serves as baseline for the articulation of the normal body" (2011, 7). But we don't just become examples of narrative prosthesis in literature. We also become examples of narrative prosthesis in the real-life stories people tell about us and themselves. A public walk is a struggle that I don't want others to witness. I don't want to become one of the neighborhood's narrative prosthetics. When Garland-Thompson writes, "The kind of staring that 'fixes' a person in gender, race, disability, class, or sexuality systems is an attempt to control the other" (2009, 43), she is concerned mostly with the dynamics between starer and subject of stares. But what about when the starer is hidden behind window blinds or curtains? When we *feel* the stares instead of seeing them, like a body in a peep show when the voyeurs are cloaked in darkened booths?

Besides the reflex to run from public pity, trauma also keeps me in the house. "Let it be recognized," Tobin Siebers notes, "that physical barriers are each and every one of them physic barriers as well" (2011, 51). I feel so out of place in this suburban order—and even in the town most of the time, however liberal it may be. I am the fetish and the taboo, at once, twicefold. Once I leave my house, I feel stranded, in danger and endangered. Not only am I black, in a time in which the epidemic of Jim Crow has spread across the country with no vaccine in sight, but I am "autistic while black" and also ill. Much has been written about the phenomenon of pain, but "hurt," as a separate thing, has received less attention. The hurt that lodges in your heart. The mental wound that spreads through your body and spirit like cancer. For me, black hurt, going back many generations. The blues, then, as disability. So many unfortunate things can happen in public places, even here. Confederate flags. Gunracks in pickups. Police profiling. "Accidental" bumps. The "changing sides of the street" or "speeding up the walk" thing. Country music.

* * *

It's three o'clock in the morning, and I'm sitting on the screened-in back porch listening to the sounds of my insect friends, listening to the many voices of rain. A soft rain and the different voices it takes, hitting leaves of the willow, or redbud, or crabapple, shed roof, pavers, soft grasses. And the porch roof, metal gutters, and my favorite, the metal bowl of the fire pit, singing, singing, singing. It's become a habit, lately, meeting myself here around this time. Sometimes I close my eyes and meditate. Sometimes I do a few yoga stretches. Sometimes I just sit and listen, and think for a while before going back to bed, falling back to sleep, and sleeping like a baby. Sometimes I think about the phone and Zoom conversations with my mother. With old and new friends. The lights inside my wife and children. This morning there are so many sounds of water rushing through different gutters and different parts of the gutters, the indefinite murmurs, patting, and dripping. The plaintiveness here and urgency there. I can feel the drips on my skin so vividly, I keep trying to touch them and ending up with waterless fingers. In the breaths of earthworms, mushrooms, and still-green leaves, I breathe a laughter, a joy all through me.

As long as I can feel this, life all around me, and in me, and I am inside of—nothing but life eternally that even the rot and mold and decay is inside of. As long as I am in this place of shared loss so deep the whole world feels it. But also in a place of lost, and found, as in finding a way to live each day whole in a different body. Finding new things, like a pad in my room of musical instruments. A pad that I can make songs and beats on for endless hours. As in finding joy that doesn't grin, but is still strong medicine. To mourn, but also celebrate. Even in this place and space of worry and loss. Of hurricanes or forest fires burning somewhere. Even with my inner clock out of sync and my lost sanctum. Even bumping into things, dropping things, and the country falling apart. Even the cracks in the foundation and waters bursting through. Even the mournful cries of songbirds. Even the fatigue and aging and aching body. Even in this pandemic on this crooked Earth. Even in this place inside of so many dangerous places, inside so many different places. At least, some of the time, I will be okay.

Works Cited

Clare, Eli. 2015. *Exile and Pride: Disability, Queerness, and Liberation*. Durham: Duke University Press.

Davis, Lennard J. 2002. *Bending Over Backwards: Disability, Dismodernism and Other Difficult Positions*. New York: New York University Press.

Garland-Thompson, Rosemarie. 1997. *Extraordinary Bodies: Figuring Physical Disability in American Culture and Literature*. New York: Columbia University Press.

———. 2009. *Staring: How We Look*. New York: Oxford University Press.

Mitchell, David T., and Sharon L. Snyder. 2011. *Narrative Prosthesis: Disability and the Dependencies of Discourse*. Ann Arbor: University of Michigan Press.

Siebers, Tobin. 2011. *Disability Theory*. Ann Arbor: University of Michigan Press.

Index

A
Ableism, 3, 48
Accessibility, 42
Accessible, 42
Accommodation, 49
American Sign Language (ASL), 43, 47, 49, 121
Americans with Disabilities Act (ADA), 10
Architecture, 5
Assistive technology, 55
Audubon Society's *Nature Guides: Deserts*, 33, 39
Auslan, 119, 121

B
Bauman, H-Dirksen L., 116, 121
Bérubé, Michael, 138
Boys, Jos, 132, 133

C
Clare, Eli, 5, 48, 120, 124, 154
Clark, John Lee, 48

COVID-19, 13, 54, 55, 58, 72, 78, 100, 118, 146, 148, 159
Cripistemology, 3

D
Davis, Lennard J., 161
Deaf gain, 121
De Bono, Edward, 58
De Certeau, Michel, 19
Disability paradox, 14
Disability Rights Movement, 10
Disability Studies and Critical Race Theory in Education (DisCrit), 97
Dolmage, Jay, 132

E
Education for All Handicapped Children Act, 63

F
Foucault, Michel, 85
Free Appropriate Public Education (FAPE), 97

G

Garland-Thompson, Rosemarie, 3, 162
Gilroy, Paul, 87

H

Hearing aids, 43
Hede, Paul, 21

I

Impairment, 12
Individuals with Disabilities Education Improvement Act (IDEIA), 97

J

Juvenile Rheumatoid Arthritis (JRA), 36

K

Kafer, Alison, 20, 125

L

Laing, R. D., 143
Lynch, Kevin, 18

M

Medical model, 3
Mitchell, David T., 162
Mobility, 30
Murray, Joseph J., 116, 121

N

Narrative normalcy, 65
Narrative prosthesis, 162
National Council on Disability (NCD), 54

O

ONTrackNY, 76

P

Pallasmaa, Juhani, 90
Price, Margaret, 132

R

RH incompatibility, 29
Ricoeur, Paul, 87, 88

S

Siebers, Tobin, 70, 97, 162
Sign languages, 119
Snyder, Sharon L., 162
Social model, 3
Soja, Edward, 19
Swett, William, 42

T

Thoreau, Henry David, 50
Titchkosky, Tanya, 137

U

Usher syndrome, 141

W

Wright, Frank Lloyd, 22

X

X-linked hypophosphatemia (XLH), 29

GPSR Compliance
The European Union's (EU) General Product Safety Regulation (GPSR) is a set of rules that requires consumer products to be safe and our obligations to ensure this.

If you have any concerns about our products, you can contact us on

ProductSafety@springernature.com

In case Publisher is established outside the EU, the EU authorized representative is:

Springer Nature Customer Service Center GmbH
Europaplatz 3
69115 Heidelberg, Germany

www.ingramcontent.com/pod-product-compliance
Lightning Source LLC
LaVergne TN
LVHW022039260326
834688LV00061B/977

*9 7 8 3 0 3 1 4 1 2 1 8 9 *